Was Jesus

a

New Age

Guru?

Reinventing Jesus, vol 1

Was Jesus a New Age Guru?

KIM MICHAELS

Copyright © 2013 Kim Michaels. All rights reserved. No part of this book may be used, reproduced, translated, electronically stored or transmitted by any means except by written permission from the publisher. A reviewer may quote brief passages in a review.

MORE TO LIFE PUBLISHING

www.morepublish.com

For foreign and translation rights,

contact info@ morepublish.com

ISBN: 978-9949-518-36-4

Series ISBN: 978-9949-518-35-7

The information and insights in this book should not be considered as a form of therapy, advice, direction, diagnosis, and/or treatment of any kind. This information is not a substitute for medical, psychological, or other professional advice, counseling and care. All matters pertaining to your individual health should be supervised by a physician or appropriate health-care practitioner. No guarantee is made by the author or the publisher that the practices described in this book will yield successful results for anyone at any time. They are presented for informational purposes only, as the practice and proof rests with the individual.

CONTENTS

Introduction to the Reinventing Jesus Series 7
Introduction to this Book 15
1 | Is Jesus Obsolete? 21
2 | From Fear to Love 27
3 | Is the Bible Relevant to Modern People? 41
4 | How Did Jesus Teach His Disciples? 51
5 | How the Official Jesus Was Invented 59
6 | No More Dancing around the Golden Calf 77
7 | Did Jesus Preach a Pacifying Form of Salvation? 89
8 | Did Jesus Teach Instant Salvation? 107
9 | What Kind of Teacher Was Jesus? 119
10 | Does Jesus Want Us to Attain Christ Consciousness? 137
11 Why Are We in the Death Consciousness? 155
12 | Explaining the Deeper Questions of Life 167
13 | Why Do People Leave Christianity? 177
14 | What Is Christ and Anti-Christ? 185
15 | What Is Truth? 199
16 | The Second Coming of Christ 221
Epilogue 225

Many modern people feel
that Christianity cannot meet
their spiritual needs.

❧

INTRODUCTION TO THE REINVENTING JESUS SERIES

I am not writing this series of books for people who consider themselves "good Christians." The reason being that their minds are probably closed to the kind of questions I will ask and the ideas I will present. They will most likely label these books as the works of the devil. I am writing these books for people who, like myself, have the following characteristics:

- As children we were exposed to some form of Christianity.

- We always knew in our hearts that we are spiritual people.

- We could never see the connection between our inner spirituality and the outer doctrines and dogmas of Christianity.

This caused some of us to reject all spirituality. It caused others to reject Jesus as a spiritual figure or spiritual teacher. After all, how do you separate Christ from Christianity?

This reaction is very understandable. After all, if you come to the priest with a question that is important to you and you are met with an overbearing smile and the statement: "It's a mystery, my child," then sooner or later you will stop asking. You might reason that either Christianity has no answers or you might start looking for answers elsewhere. This has caused an interesting situation:

- Many modern people feel that Christianity cannot meet their spiritual needs.

- Because they cannot separate Jesus from Christianity, they feel that Jesus probably has no answers to their spiritual questions.

I have certainly felt that way myself, but a long time ago I asked myself this question: "Why did I choose to be born in a Christian society?" I realized I had a reason for making this choice and that I owed it to myself to figure out what that reason is. I believe this question is relevant for millions of people in the modern world and it is even important for society as a whole. After all, modern civilization is facing an interesting situation.

Do people no longer have spiritual needs?

I grew up in Denmark, an affluent country with a highly developed welfare system. The result is that people can grow up

Introduction to the Reinventing Jesus Series

feeling that they don't have to worry too much about their material needs. According to the unspoken assumptions of Danish society, taking care of people's material needs should automatically make them happy.

International surveys have indeed established Denmark as the nation with the happiest people. Yet part of the welfare system is public health care and this includes mental health services. As material affluence has grown, more and more people have sought help for depression and more serious mental health problems. For my great grandparents, who had to work much harder than people do today, this was an unknown phenomenon. They simply didn't have the luxury of worrying about how they felt about life. They either bowed their heads and soldiered on or they drank themselves to death.

How do we explain that many modern nations face the problem that meeting people's material needs does not make them happy? I have a simple explanation. As long as most of our attention and energy is caught up in meeting our material needs, we don't have enough attention to think about anything else. When our material needs are met to a certain degree, we will naturally become more aware of our non-material needs. If these needs are not met, we might begin to experience depression or mental illness. What was suppressed before our material needs were met, will now surface and we cannot ignore it.

In recent years, mental health care professionals in Denmark have acknowledged that over the next several decades mental illness will be the greatest challenge to the public health care system. I believe most modern nations are facing a similar problem. I also believe this problem has no easy solution, given that the health care systems of most modern nations are based on a materialistic approach to life.

Recognizing our psycho-spiritual needs

Ask yourself a simple question: Why do people in the modern world have psychological problems? If we were – as the health care system assumes – a kind of biological robots, then taking care of our material needs should automatically make us content. Given that this does not happen, we must conclude that we are not material beings. What kind of beings are we? We are psycho-spiritual beings.

What people today call psychological problems are really psycho-spiritual problems. When our material needs are met, it is only natural that we start focusing on the deeper questions of life. We human beings have a genuine need to know who we are, to know why we are here and to feel that our lives have some kind of meaning that is important to us. It is an insult to our intelligence that both Christianity and materialism push these needs aside because their "doctrines" have no easy answers.

Here we have the essential problem of modern society: Neither Christianity nor the health care system can meet people's psycho-spiritual needs. More and more people are finding themselves between a rock and a hard spot. They have psycho-spiritual needs but because they have been so turned off by Christianity, they cannot see this religion as a way to meet those needs. When the unmet needs turn into depression or more serious problems, they turn to the mental health care profession. With its materialistic approach, it simply cannot help people with their psycho-spiritual needs.

The current approach to psychology has defined us as materialistic beings, and as such it has defined psycho-spiritual needs out of existence. Our health care system is based on identifying a problem and then dealing with the cause of that problem. The problem must have only material causes, so is it any wonder modern psychology and psychiatry cannot help people with problems that it cannot identify as material problems? How can a psycho-spiritual need have a material cause or cure? No wonder modern medicine can only offer to drug you up so you no longer feel alive. Is that really any better than people in my grandparent's generation drinking themselves to death? Have we actually made any progress over the past centuries? Yes, we have made material progress, but we obviously have not made progress in the area that really matters to us: our psycho-spiritual needs.

Using our spiritual heritage

My suggestion is simple. Modern people do have psycho-spiritual needs. Modern society will never overcome the mental health care challenge until we recognize those needs and offer people a psycho-spiritual solution. I am not saying I have a ready-made definition of how this should be done. I am, however, saying that I have personally experienced that taking care of my psycho-spiritual needs could not be done without making peace with Jesus. It is not feasible to ignore the fact that I grew up in a nation with a long spiritual heritage, a heritage that has been shaped by the Christian religion.

For me it has been extremely important to take a look at that heritage and come to realize just how different the Christian religion is from what Jesus actually tried to teach us. By coming to understand how far the mainstream Christian churches have strayed from the actual teachings of Jesus, I have come to understand why Christianity cannot meet my psycho-spiritual needs. I have also come to understand that Jesus and his actual teachings can indeed meet my psycho-spiritual needs.

I have come to see that if society is to meet the psycho-spiritual needs of its citizens, we will have to confront our

Christian heritage in a way never done before. We will have to re-discover the universal spiritual principles that Jesus actually taught and relate them to the psycho-spiritual needs that people have today. We will have to take an honest look at how the Christian religion has obscured Jesus' original teachings. We will have to understand how Christianity has added baggage that has set the stage for the psycho-spiritual problems people have today. As just one example, Christianity tells us we are sinners, but Jesus did not teach this.

Imagine that Jesus took embodiment on earth today. Would he look at our scientific knowledge, throw up his hands and say: "These people will never believe in anything spiritual, I'm outta here!" Or would he look at our situation and reinvent his teachings so they could meet our psycho-spiritual needs in today's age? I think Jesus would reinvent himself and I think that if we are to meet the psycho-spiritual needs of today's people, we will have to reinvent Jesus. It is to help bring along this process that I offer these books.

You Have No Right to Reinvent Jesus!

Was Jesus a prophet? Well, he certainly did make one prediction that has proven to be incredibly accurate: "Think not that I am come to send peace on earth: I came not to send peace, but a sword." According to various estimates, there are 20-30,000 different Christian churches and sects. They have a great variety of doctrines and interpretations—many of which are mutually exclusive. If Jesus did indeed come to stir the pot, he has been remarkably successful. In fact, the only topic that is more controversial than Jesus is the topic of God.

The result is that no matter what you say about Jesus, you can be sure someone will be violently opposed to it. This means it is predictable that some people will have a strong reaction to

Introduction to the Reinventing Jesus Series

the title of this series. Some might say: "How dare you think you have the right to reinvent Jesus? Our church has the only truth about Jesus, and you have no right to come here and say people are free to reinvent Jesus in the modern world. That is blasphemy and will send you straight to hell."

My response to that sentiment is that such people apparently don't know much about the history of their religion. If you do know the basic facts about the history of Christianity, you know that the Jesus we have inherited is not the Jesus who walked the earth 2,000 years ago. Instead, we have been handed down a Jesus who was invented in the ancient world, especially after Christianity became the official religion of the Roman empire. The Jesus who was invented in the ancient world was clearly designed based on what was common knowledge back then. Perhaps this explains why the ancient Jesus no longer has the same appeal to people in the modern world? Why wouldn't it be perfectly logical to reinvent Jesus based on what we know in the modern world? Why wouldn't we reinvent Jesus so that his teachings can better address the psycho-spiritual needs we have in the modern world?

A practical note

One practical note about these books. We live in a society where people have more free time than ever, yet people still feel they never have enough time. These books are written to be as short and succinct as possible. This means each book will focus on a clearly defined topic without going into a deeper philosophical discussion about all aspects of Christianity or spirituality. In order to make the books easier to read in short segments, they have been organized as a series of clearly defined ideas. You can read one idea before you go to sleep or while you are commuting to work.

What Christianity is doing today
is ignoring the obvious progress
that humankind has made
over the past 2,000 years.

INTRODUCTION TO THIS BOOK

It has always been curious to me that so many Christians are convinced that their particular church has the only true way to look at Jesus and his teachings. The underlying assumption seems to be that it is easy for people to grasp who Jesus was and what he taught. All that is required is that you accept a few doctrines and interpretations and then you have – supposedly – grasped all you need to know about Jesus. I personally think this is an incredible arrogance on our part.

I have studied the topic of Jesus and his teachings from many different angles over a period of more than 30 years. I do not in any way claim that I understand the fullness of who Jesus is and what he is seeking to teach us. In fact, I sometimes feel the truth in the old statement that the more I know, the more I realize I don't know. To me, it is arrogant to think we can easily grasp Jesus' message. I think his message is complex and multi-faceted with different layers. In order to grasp it, we have to go through a long and gradual process of opening our minds to a higher perspective, even a higher state of consciousness. This brings me to the title of this book.

I have met many Christians who believe that if they had been alive 2,000 years ago, they would have instantly recognized and accepted Jesus. I find this highly unlikely. If you look at the scriptures, it becomes clear that most people at the time did not see Jesus as a significant spiritual figure. Why not?

One reason is that back then most people were following the mainstream religion of their culture and Jesus was by no means a mainstream preacher. Jesus was constantly opposed and denounced by those who represented the mainstream religion of the time. Why did they oppose him? Because he had a message that went far beyond their doctrines and they saw him as a threat to their control over the people.

Jesus was rejected by the closed-minded religious people of this time, those who thought that accepting a few doctrines and following a few rules was enough to get them to heaven. They accused him of blasphemy and called him all kinds of names. What would these people have called Jesus if they had used today's terminology? I believe they would have called him a dangerous New Age cult leader. After all, he did tell his followers to leave everything behind in order to follow him, even to be willing to lose their lives for his sake.

Instant oatmeal and instant salvation

In my experience, most Christians have never considered that Jesus was rejected by those who followed the mainstream religion of his time. They have never considered that they themselves are following the mainstream religion of *their* time. They have never considered that Jesus was a radical preacher, meaning that those who follow any mainstream religion will likely reject his real message. As I said, Jesus was rejected by the closed-minded religious people of his time. Who are the closed-minded religious people of today? Well, in all honesty, many Christians are among them.

Most Christians would likely reject Jesus if he walked the earth today. They would likely fail to recognize his true message because they think it is too radical. They would prefer the message preached by mainstream Christianity and they would fail to see just how different it is from the message presented by Jesus.

In a time when instant gratification has become the de facto religion, it is perhaps no wonder that so many Christians believe in instant salvation. I see this as a result of the fact that for over 1600 years Christianity has preached that salvation is a matter of accepting the doctrines and following the rules of an external religion. This belief has been combined with the mindset produced by modern technology, namely the belief that if you push the right button, the result follows mechanically.

Many people believe that if they live up to a set of outer requirements defined by their church, their salvation is automatic and guaranteed. They believe that if they push the right buttons, Jesus simply *has* to show up at their funeral and take them to heaven.

I think this is a completely fictional image of salvation and it blatantly ignores, dis-interprets, covers over and explains away the form of salvation that Jesus actually taught. Jesus did *not* teach an instant, automatic or guaranteed salvation. He taught that *salvation is a process!*

The core of this process is that you raise your state of consciousness to a level that is fundamentally different from what most human beings call normal. The state of consciousness that Jesus wants us to attain is so far above normal that it is almost impossible for us to grasp the difference with our present level of awareness.

Jesus taught that salvation is a gradual process. You cannot instantly shift your consciousness, so you go through a process of progressively more complex initiations. This is the process that Jesus was giving to his disciples.

Why was Jesus' original message lost?

In the following chapters I will comment on why Jesus' original message has been lost. At this point I want to briefly mention one of the reasons, namely that his message is not easy to grasp. Jesus himself was apparently aware of this. The scriptures tell us that Jesus taught the multitudes in parables and only when they were alone together did he "expound all things to his disciples."

I see this as a clear indication that Jesus was aware that back then the majority of the people were not ready for his real message. They were not ready to engage in a gradual path of initiation, leading to a radically different state of consciousness. He therefore gave them a set of parables and commandments that were designed to challenge them to raise their consciousness until they were ready for the inner path.

Have you ever considered what it would take to truly follow the call to turn the other cheek? Would it not take a shift into a state of consciousness that is radically different from what we call normal human awareness? Would it not require you to truly understand what Jesus meant with his cryptic statement that you must remove the beam from your own eye? If people had taken Jesus' outer teachings and had accepted the challenge to fully embody them, they would gradually have come to see the need to change their state of consciousness.

Instead, what happened was that the same mindset that dominated the Jewish religion took over the Christian movement. This mindset said that what keeps you out of heaven is your sins, which are partly the result of the actions you have taken. You can compensate for your bad actions by performing good actions, such as sacrificing animals. You can gain entry into heaven without changing your state of consciousness. As I will explain in greater depth, it was this outer path to salvation that came to dominate the Christian religion, and it has done so ever since.

Why people look beyond Christianity

For centuries, this outer approach to salvation seemed to satisfy most people and they never revolted against mainstream Christianity. Yet why are more and more people leaving Christianity in this age? I think it is because people are intuitively sensing that the outer path simply isn't enough, it cannot meet our psycho-spiritual needs. The only way to truly answer our questions about life and its meaning is to raise our consciousness so that we can see something we do not grasp today.

I know that both mainstream Christians and scientific materialists have nothing but contempt for the phenomenon labeled as "New Age." Yet if you go back to Jesus' own time, you see that there was also great diversity in the spiritual field. Christianity has led us to believe that there were only Jews and Christians, but the picture was far more complex with many sects and preachers. This is exactly what we see today, and my conclusion is that we live in a time when there is great opportunity for spiritual growth.

Many people feel an inner urge to find answers to their psycho-spiritual questions, but because they cannot find answers in Christianity, they either feel like they have nowhere to go or they look to a variety of New Age or Eastern gurus. I see that we live in an age when many people are ready for the higher path that Jesus taught to his disciples. I think it is highly ironic that the religion that claims to represent Jesus cannot offer these people the path taught by Jesus himself.

I think we need to make an effort to correct this by reinventing Jesus as what he really was: a spiritual teacher who taught and demonstrated a gradual path of initiation leading to a radically higher state of consciousness.

I fully realize this is a rather ambitious goal, so let me provide a more gradual approach for those who have grown up in a Christian culture and have not yet considered some of its shortcomings. I will build gradually towards an explanation of the path and the state of consciousness that Jesus truly came to give as his gift to humankind.

1 | IS JESUS OBSOLETE?

Why are people leaving Christianity?

No matter what you say about Jesus or Christianity, someone will disagree with it. You can indeed find Christian ministers who deny that Christianity is a religion in crisis. Some say it is a growing religion and they refer to new converts being added in Africa and Asia.

This book is for people who realize that in most of the older Christian countries, people are leaving Christian churches in droves. Who can deny that the sexual abuse of children by Catholic priests – and the Church's systematic attempts at covering it up – has caused large numbers of people to leave the Catholic Church? Who can deny that in most European countries, in Canada and even in the United States, Christian churches are shrinking and societies are becoming more and more secularized? Who can deny that while this trend has been going on for almost a century, it has clearly accelerated in the last few years?

As I said in the introduction, modern people do indeed have psycho-spiritual needs. There is only one reason they would choose to leave: Christianity is no longer meeting people's needs. This leads to a clear conclusion:

If Christianity is to survive in the modern world, it will have to find a way to meet people's needs. How could that be done without reinventing Jesus?

Top-down or user-friendly?

In my observation, the one area of society that is best at adapting to changes is the business world. It is all due to that supply and demand thing and competition. If people don't need what you are selling, you must either sell something else or go out of business. Perhaps the market fundamentals also work in the area of religion?

When I grew up, Danish radio and television had a monopoly position. There was only one Danish television channel and three radio channels—you simply couldn't get any other channels. The people running the show knew they had a captive audience, and they saw it as their role to define what the Danish people should want to receive. It was a top-down approach where the people in charge had little need to pay attention to those on the receiving end. They did indeed pay very little attention, seeing themselves as a kind of gods who could define what type of culture people should have. The result being, of course that people became apathetic, either taking whatever was offered or simply pushing the "Off" button.

That all changed in the 1970s, partly due to pressure from the people and partly due to certain technological advances, especially cable television. As soon as people could receive Swedish or German TV, the monopoly was broken. And then TV and radio started having call-in programs, more game shows with ordinary people as participants and more interviews with non-celebrities. They even started doing customer surveys, asking people what they thought about present offerings and what they wanted.

If you look at the business world, you will see that something similar has happened over the past several decades. The most successful businesses are those who understand how to build relationships with their customers. They do surveys to find out how people use existing products and they try to anticipate people's needs. They place a high priority on good customer service. Some businesses, such as Apple, have become good at seeing needs that no one has ever articulated before. How many consumers had been lying awake at night longing for a phone with a touchscreen before the iPhone appeared? Once it was there, the unaddressed need became obvious.

How does Christianity stack up in the customer service department? How does the Christian religion score in terms of user-friendliness? How has the Christian religion done in terms of identifying people's needs and adapting its product offerings to meet those needs? To me, the loss of membership says it all.

Is Christianity a user-friendly religion?

One of the most stunning customer-relations failures in the history of the human race must surely be the way the Catholic Church handled the sexual abuse issue. For decades, church leaders knew there was a problem with a minority of priests systematically abusing children. What was the most common response? When complaints started to come in about a certain priest, he was moved to another parish where he had a fresh supply of victims. The parents of the victims were intimidated into silence. If you believe your church has the power to send you to heaven or condemn you to hell, well, you really don't want to make too many waves, do you?

Another stunning failure is that Christianity as a religion has not renewed its product offering for centuries. The

Catholic Church is the oldest mainstream Christian denomination. Many of its doctrines were set in stone at the Council of Nicaea—*which took place in the year 325.* It was there that Jesus – likely to his great surprise – found himself elevated to the status of being the *only* Son of God, thereby being set apart from all other human beings.

Some Lutheran Christians might snicker at this, thinking they are far more modern. Yet when Luther nailed his 95 Theses to that church door in 1517, he identified certain elements that the Catholic Church had added to Christianity and he later removed them. What he did not do was to put back in what the Catholic church fathers had taken out centuries earlier. Luther didn't do this because he couldn't. He simply had no way of knowing what was taken out during the process of reinventing Christianity as the official religion of the Roman empire. Even today, we don't know the full story, but at least we know a lot more than Luther did.

Despite the fact that the scientific method has expanded our understanding of Christianity's history no Christian church has dared to step back and ask the question: "Are our product offerings out of touch with the psycho-spiritual needs of today's people?"

Nor have many people dared to consider that perhaps Christianity is out of touch with the times because it is dragging along a heritage from the far-distant past. Perhaps it is this heritage that makes it nigh-impossible for Christianity to adapt to the changing times and the changing needs of the people? We no longer accept the idea that one political leader, namely the emperor, is God on earth. Yet we still drag along the clearly Roman baggage that Jesus was fundamentally different from the rest of us.

Take note that I am not hereby ignoring the fact that many individual pastors of Christian churches have done a lot to adapt their religion to the needs of their congregations. One example is youth programs where pastors adapt their preaching style and music selection to the needs of young people. What I am talking about here is the big picture, which is beyond the reach of individual pastors. I am talking about everything from the obvious doctrines to the not-so-obvious world-view that Christianity has inherited from the past. So far, no Christian church has dared to truly step back and look at the history of Christianity, asking what we are dragging along that became outdated centuries ago.

Change does not come from the top

What I will do in this and coming books in the series is to step back and look at the big picture. I will ask some of the many questions that few if any Christians have asked—and that many church leaders would consider forbidden or blasphemous questions. Yet if we don't ask the questions, how can we ever adapt to a changing society? If Christianity doesn't adapt, how will it avoid becoming as the dinosaurs—whose existence some Christian ministers deny to this day?

I write this book for two reasons. One is that I love Jesus; not as some idol hanging in a church, but as a real, living spiritual being. I think Jesus deserves to have a far better outcome of his efforts to enlighten humankind.

The other reason I step forward is that I know enough about history to see that positive change rarely comes from the top down—it usually comes from the bottom up. The reason is that leaders tend to hold on to their positions. They seek to prevent any change that they see as a threat—and some see *any* change as a threat. Change does not happen until a critical pressure has been created from below whereby it becomes clear that the people will no longer accept business as usual.

Jesus' own life demonstrates that he did not believe change would come from the leaders. He attempted to appeal directly to the people.

It is clear to me that unless Christianity goes through a radical change, it will not survive as a major religion. It is equally clear that such a change will not come from the top—because then it should have happened decades or even centuries ago. The only realistic potential is that enough people stand up and demand a new form of Christianity, thereby either creating new types of Christian churches or forcing the old ones to reinvent themselves. The problem being, of course, that right now people can't stand up and demand anything. They have no say in their churches. They can only stand up and walk out—*and many do.*

Let us imagine that you go along with this idea and say: "Okay, but then show me what kind of changes you think need to happen?" This is precisely what I will do in this and coming books. What I can say already is that the changes will be based on the realization that we need to deepen our understanding of who Jesus was and what he actually taught. It is obvious to me that there is no way to relate the official image of Christ with the psycho-spiritual needs of today's people. If we are to meet the needs of modern people, we simply have to reinvent Jesus.

I can crystallize my sentiment in this simple question: "What is it that is becoming obsolete: Is it Jesus or the image of Jesus presented by Christianity?" Or we might ask: "Which Jesus is becoming obsolete: the Jesus invented by the Christian religion or the real Jesus?"

2 | FROM FEAR TO LOVE

Fear simply has to go

As a child I read a novel about stone-age people. The point that stuck in my mind was that according to the author, people back then were afraid to leave their houses at night because they thought evil spirits would get them. Obviously, the author couldn't possibly know this, but he based it on what we know about native tribes. I also remember reading about the beliefs of medieval people who thought werewolves, dragons and witches were very real threats. I think it is obvious that people in the past were afraid of many things that we simply laugh at today. If you set up a fear barometer, it would have gone down a lot compared to what people believed when Christian doctrines were set in ink.

Despite the obvious fact that modern people have less fear, we still have a Christianity that has an incredible amount of fear-based doctrines and beliefs. In my observation, this form of Christianity no longer appeals to the majority of modern people.

I have met fundamentalist Christians in the United States who think people in Europe are not God-fearing, and I believe they are right. The vast majority of the people in Europe have long ago grown away from the kind of fears that appealed to people in medieval times. This means that a fear-based Christianity that appealed to people in centuries past simply cannot reach people in the modern world.

I think we need to acknowledge the fact that the Christianity we have inherited was designed to appeal to people whose main concern in life was to avoid spending eternity being tormented in a fiery hell. Given that most modern people have transcended that fear, how can Christianity possibly appeal to them in its present form?

This leads to what is one of the major challenges facing Christianity today, namely how to reinvent Christianity based on the fact that people simply no longer have the fears that led to or were induced by some of the major Christian doctrines. The challenge is to move away from a fear-based approach to religion and move towards a love-based approach.

Fear-based Christianity suppressing the people

When I was a boy during the 1960s, most people in Denmark had long ago grown away from a fear-based approach to religion. I know some Christian ministers will blame this on science and materialism, but I think that is only part of the answer. A factor that I rarely see mentioned in this context is the advent of democracy. Before democracy, people in Denmark (and of course many other nations) were living in constant fear of their overlords. When democracy became a reality, much of this fear dissipated, and that meant people started to outgrow all kinds of fears.

I believe that in the late 1800s Christianity had a golden opportunity to reinvent itself so it was no longer a fear-based religion. Since that opportunity was passed by, people in many democratic countries simply abandoned a Christianity that no longer appealed to them. After all, it doesn't take a genius to see that before the advent of democracy, fear-based Christianity had very much been part of the power apparatus that suppressed the people.

Medieval Christianity tied in to the fact that people were suffering in their daily lives. They were suffering because they lived in an elitist society where a small upper class had the majority of the wealth and privileges. This caused a focus on the suffering of Jesus, which was given the twist that suffering in this world could lead to a better status in the coming world. Coupled with the fear of hell, this became a very efficient "force" for maintaining the status quo where the members of a small elite were able to control the population.

It is a historical fact that for centuries there was an uneasy alliance between Christianity and the kings, emperors and noblemen of Europe. The Church made it clear that rebelling against its authority could lead to an eternity in hell. If the Church supported a king, the signal was that rebelling against the king was the same as rebelling against God.

At the same time as the Church was raising this stick, it also held out a carrot. If only you endured suffering in *this* world, as Jesus had done, you would be rewarded by God in *the next* world. The underlying message was clear: Even though your earthly overlords are suppressing you, rebelling against them will lead you to hell whereas accepting your suffering in this world will bring you rewards in the next world. Is it really any wonder that when dictatorial rulers were replaced by democracy, the fear-based Christianity that had supported the old rulers also lost its appeal? When the general amount of fear was reduced, how could a fear-based Christianity continue to have a hold on people? Of course, not all people in democratic countries have transcended a fear-based approach to life.

The fear versus no fear dilemma

Although I grew up in Denmark, I lived in the United States for 22 years. It has been my experience that in Europe, especially in Northern Europe, a fear-based religion appeals to only a small fraction of the population. In the United States fear-based religion appeals to a significantly larger part of the population, as witnessed by the amount of Christian fundamentalist churches. In my observation, a majority of Americans have transcended a fear-based approach to life, but it is a smaller percentage than in Europe. There are still enough people who take a fear-based approach to religion that it presents Christianity with a rather tricky dilemma.

What is the essence of fear? There must be an external factor that you see as a threat, and then there must be something that gives you refuge against that threat. Medieval Christianity defined the external factor as a devil who was seeking to drag you to an eternity of torment in hell, and your only refuge was the church. The effect being, or course that people tried to avoid the threat and cling to the refuge. Say you are walking in the mountains and slip, suddenly finding yourself clinging to a rope over an abyss. Would you not cling to that rope for as long as you possibly could? Is this not precisely the reaction of many Christians today?

We can now define three types of reactions to life. I did not receive what would traditionally be called a religious upbringing, but I can assure you that the hellfire and brimstone variant of Christianity would have had no chance of appealing to me whatsoever. As a child (or later for that matter) I never doubted that God exists, but I also was absolutely sure that my God is a loving God. The idea that this God would send me to hell for disobeying a church on earth simply did not compute.

For the past 36 years, I have been on a personal quest to get to know this loving God. In the process I have met thousands of people who could be characterized by a statement that has become common in recent years: "I am spiritual, but not religious." This leads me to the three typical reactions to religion:

- Many people have an interest in the spiritual side of life but have completely outgrown fear-based religion. Given that Christianity is still so steeped in fear, most of them have seen no other way than to steer clear of their childhood religion.

- Another group of people are those with little interest or belief in spiritual matters. If you try to talk to them about spiritual topics, you will get complete indifference or even hostility. As I was growing up, most of my family members were in this category, as was the majority of the Danish population. The same is true for the majority of the population in Europe and a large number of people in the United States.

- Finally, we have people who do believe in God, but who take a fear-based approach. Many of these are indeed active members of various Christian churches and they often believe Christianity is under threat. What is their reaction? They first of all believe their approach to religion is right, and thus they often seek leadership positions in Christian churches. Because they are driven by a certain zeal and willingness to make sacrifices, they often attain such positions. Once there, they do exactly as the person hanging on to a rope over an abyss: they hold on for dear life.

Let us imagine that Christianity was to reinvent itself and make the transition from a fear-based to a love-based religion. Who are the people that could initiate and complete this process? Well, it certainly won't be the large part of the population who are indifferent or hostile towards religion. It could potentially be done by the many people who have already shifted into a love-based approach to spirituality, but most of them wouldn't touch a Christian church with a ten-foot pole. The reason is that they simply don't want to deal with the fear-based Christians who think it is their sacred duty to preserve a fear-based Christianity. Obviously, the fear-based people could not transform Christianity into a love-based religion even if they wanted to.

Christianity is not only a religion in crisis; it is a religion that is in a catch-22, a so-called non-resolvable dilemma. Is there a way out? As I have already said, it certainly will not come from the fear-based leaders. The remaining question is whether there are enough Christians who have shifted or are willing to shift into a love-based approach and then demand change from below? Are there enough people who will speak out instead of standing by and watching the Christian religion move closer and closer to oblivion? At this point, I really have no answer to that question.

Was Jesus a hellfire and brimstone preacher?

As mentioned, there are thousands of Christian churches, and many of them are convinced that they are the only true Christian church. Many of the leaders and members of such churches seem to be absolutely sure that if Jesus himself walked into their church on any given Sunday, he would be in complete agreement with everything that is going on there. They must assume that Jesus was the exact same kind of preacher as the one standing in their pulpit every Sunday. But is that a realistic assumption?

Let us be more specific. Is it realistic to assume that because there are many hellfire and brimstone preachers in Christian churches, Jesus himself was also a hellfire and brimstone preacher? Does the fact that Christianity has taken a fear-based approach to religion mean that Jesus himself also took a fear-based approach? Did Jesus actually want to start a fear-based religion?

This is a big topic, but for now let us just look at a couple of simple hints. If you search an online version of the New Testament, you will find that the word "hell" appears 23 times. The word "fear" appears 78 times, but if you then start reading, you realize that in 27 cases, the word "fear" is followed by the word "not," as in "fear not." Here are just a few statements that actually deny a fear-based approach to religion:

> Fear not, little flock; for it is your Father's good pleasure to give you the kingdom. (Luke 12:32)

> For God hath not given us the spirit of fear; but of power, and of love, and of a sound mind. (2 Timothy 1:7)

> There is no fear in love; but perfect love casteth out fear: because fear hath torment. He that feareth is not made perfect in love. (1 John 4:18)

Just look at that last statement. Isn't it a stunning concept to be "made perfect in love?" Doesn't it just send shivers up and down your spine? Of course, we also have a very telling situation where Jesus is challenged by the hellfire and brimstone preachers of the Jewish religion. They seek to trap him by asking him what is the most important commandments of the law. Jesus answers:

> Thou shalt love the Lord thy God with all thy heart, and with all thy soul, and with all thy mind. (Matthew 22:37)

As most psychologists will tell you, love and fear are incompatible emotions. You cannot truly love something that you fear. It is impossible to love God with all your "heart, soul and mind" if you fear that this same God will send you to eternal torment in hell if you don't love him. You simply cannot be scared into loving someone.

If you search the New Testament for the word love, it appears 202 times. We see at least a hint that Jesus himself did not attempt to motivate his followers through fear. He seems to have attempted to give them a love-based motivation for approaching God.

Cause, effect and fear

I earlier said that the fear barometer has gone down in the modern world compared to previous centuries. One of the major reasons for this is, of course, science. At this point I don't want to go into a deeper discussion of the relationship between Christianity and science because it's a big topic that I want to save for some later time. What I want to focus on here is why science has enabled us to overcome many of the fears people had in previous ages.

The main reason for this is that science has taught us a very simple concept: cause and effect. If you look at the psychological effect of fear, you will see that most of our fears are related to the realm of effect. We are not afraid of the bacteria that cause a disease; we are afraid of the pain or death that is the effect of the disease.

We can now combine this with the simple fact that our greatest fears are related to the unknown. For example, not many people in the modern world go around fearing pneumonia. Yet a little over a century ago, most people were very scared of pneumonia because it was a common disease and it was almost always fatal. Since then, scientists discovered that pneumonia is caused by a certain type of bacteria, and by using Penicillin it is possible to kill that bacteria, causing most people to survive.

Take note of the deeper aspect here. Pneumonia was scary when we only knew the effect and did not know the cause. If you do not know the cause, you have no chance of doing anything to avoid the effect. Once you do understand the cause of a phenomenon, your fear of the effect is either reduced or it simply evaporates.

There is absolutely no way to undo the psychological impact that the knowledge of cause and effect has had on people. We will never go back to a situation where people have the same fears as people had during the Middle Ages. You cannot turn back the clock—and why would you want to? This is another reason fear-based religion will have little appeal to modern people.

Think back to medieval Christianity. People were taught to fear God because if they didn't, they would go to hell. Yet they were not even allowed to read the Bible for themselves, as it could not be translated from Latin. What you had in medieval times was the typical relationship between fear and the unknown. People were told to fear God, but they were not told exactly why. They were taught about the effect – burning forever in hell – but they were not taught why a supposedly good God might want them to burn in hell, or why he would create them as sinners so they would have a high probability of ending up in hell.

All I am trying to say here is simply this: The cat's out of the bag! No amount of hellfire and brimstone preaching will return us to a state where you can motivate people to believe in God out of fear. In today's world, most people will not be content with a religion that only tells them about effects. If you can't come up with a reasonable explanation of cause, then you might as well give up trying.

My Catholic friends tell me that the standard reaction from their priests was: "It's a mystery." Well, that simply won't cut it in a world that is aware of cause and effect. If you ask people to believe something or follow certain rituals, but you can't explain to them the cause behind it, you have no chance of reaching modern people. They will ask themselves: "Why should I bother going to church when no one can explain why?"

What would Jesus do?

From time to time, churches in the United States make an attempt to promote the concept: "What would Jesus do?" The idea is to get people to make personal decisions based on how Jesus would have handled a given situation. Apparently, such churches don't find it necessary to apply this consideration to themselves or to the Christian religion in general. What would Jesus do about the psycho-spiritual needs of people in the modern world?

If Jesus walked the earth today, don't you think he would have made use of the fact that people know a lot more about the world than people did 2,000 years ago? Do you really think Jesus would have been intimidated or silenced by scientific materialists? Don't you think he would have made use of the findings of science in order to explain to people what he simply had no way of explaining two millennia ago? Do you think Jesus would have engaged in a battle with science or have told his followers to ignore scientific findings? Or do you think he would have embraced the opportunity to explain much more than could be explained back then?

Clearly, a fear-based Jesus would indeed battle with science, and he would use fear to intimidate Christians into denying science and upholding the literal interpretation of the Bible. I personally can't see a love-based Jesus being intimidated by anything that materialism can come up with. After all, Jesus knows from direct experience that there is something beyond the material world.

The bottom line is simply this: My vision is that Jesus does indeed have cause-and-effect teachings about every aspect of our psycho-spiritual needs. I see many Christians who – without realizing this – fear that such answers don't exist. I also see the reality that there are indeed answers, but modern Christians simply can't see them. The reason is that they are looking through a filter created by Christianity itself.

The problem is that this filter was created centuries ago when people didn't know what we know today. The effect is that in order to uphold the filter, you have to deny or ignore a lot of modern knowledge. As long as you deny modern knowledge, how can you adapt Christianity to this knowledge and meet people's needs? Another closed circle, a serpent biting its own tail, a catch-22.

The loss shall set you free

What will it take for you to move into a new phase? It will take that you let go of the old. Fear causes us to cling to the old. What will it take to let go of the old? It will take love; you must love something more than the old. When you acknowledge your love for the new, letting go of the old comes naturally and effortlessly. After all, it is holding on that requires effort whereas letting go requires the cessation of effort.

The question one might ask is what Christians truly love? Many will claim to love Jesus, but which Jesus do they love? Do they love the Jesus that was invented by Christianity in a distant past—the fear-based Jesus? Or do they love the living Jesus, the spiritual being who cannot be confined to any doctrines or dogmas here on earth? Or do they actually love an earthly institution, the church, with all its pomp and circumstance and the promise of certainty?

If Christianity is to move from a fear-based to a love-based approach, this will have to be facilitated by people who love something more than the old. In loving something more, they are willing to look at the old and let go of those elements that have simply become obsolete.

When you love something more, you are willing to endure the loss of the old. In fact, people cling to the old because they feel that letting go of it can only lead to loss. When you truly love, you will not even feel that letting go of the old is a loss. You gain so much more by embracing the new. There are some "losses" that will actually set you free from the limitations of the old.

Reach back to my example of a person walking in the mountains who suddenly finds himself hanging on to a rope over what he thinks is an abyss. He closes his eyes and hangs on for dear life, until he suddenly feels a gentle tap on his shoulder and hears a voice saying: "Hey, your feet are 10 centimeters above the rocky ledge upon which I am standing. Let go of the rope and let's walk out of here." Would letting go of the rope be a loss, or would it set him free from a very tense situation that truly imprisoned him?

In my observation many Christians are in a very strained and tense situation, and it is because they are seeking to hold on to the old. By simply taking a look and acknowledging what needs to change, it is not that hard to transcend the tension.

How can knowledge cause a loss of faith?

I know, of course, what the primary objection will be. Many Christians fear that if they do take a look, they will lose their faith. Let me point out a very simple mechanism: What imprisons you is an illusion because the truth can only set you free.

What you are clinging to is always an illusion. If you come to see it as an illusion, you will not lose faith; you will gain a higher form of faith, one that is not based on belief but on knowing. As we will see later, that just might be exactly what Jesus wanted for all of his followers.

If you come to see that what you have believed so far is an illusion, then that means you must also see a higher truth. How can you come to realize that something is an illusion unless you also see a higher truth? How can seeing a higher truth cause you to lose anything? You can only gain by seeing a higher truth, which means you can only gain by looking.

I fully realize that this line of reasoning will have no impact on a person trapped in fear. Yet this book is not written for such people, for how could I possibly help those who have allowed their fears to close their minds? You might notice that Jesus himself often called for those who had ears to hear or eyes to see. He obviously acknowledged that some people are beyond reach. I certainly would not profess to think I can help those whom Jesus himself could not reach.

Let us move on to look at some of the things that we have to be willing to lose in order to move from a fear-based to a love-based form of Christianity.

Jesus respected the existing tradition,
but not to the point where he wanted
that tradition to be used
as a weapon against renewal.

3 | IS THE BIBLE RELEVANT TO MODERN PEOPLE?

Was Jesus a Bible-thumper?

One of the things that turns a lot of people off to official Christianity is the tendency to use Bible quotes to intimidate people into silence. So many Christians and Christian preachers will quote scripture in order to prove their point or to disprove some question you might have. This is especially a turn-off when the quote doesn't actually prove a certain point, but only "proves" it when interpreted in a special way—which the person will say is the only true way to interpret it.

This almost fanatical insistence on the Bible being the ultimate authority for all spiritual questions is part of the legacy that official Christianity has inherited from the past. Given that the New Testament was written down almost 2,000 years ago, is it realistic that it should be able to answer all questions about spirituality we have in the modern world?

If we are to meet the psycho-spiritual needs of today's people, we need more openness and flexibility. We need to accept other sources of knowledge than the Bible. We need to open up to a more flexible interpretation of the inner, spiritual meaning of many teachings found in the official scriptures. We might start this process by considering whether Jesus used religious scriptures the same way as the people who claim to represent Jesus in the modern world. In other words, was Jesus a Bible-thumper?

Well, of course that question is ridiculous because the Bible that we know today didn't exist at Jesus' time. Yet there was an official scripture, namely the Jewish scriptures of the Torah. Was Jesus a "Torah-thumper?" Not hardly.

In fact, Jesus was constantly being attacked by the Bible-thumpers of his day, namely the scribes and Pharisees. They repeatedly attempted to use the scriptures against Jesus, saying that because he did or said this or that, he could not be the Messiah. In the Gospel of Matthew, Jesus' response is rather telling: "Woe unto you, scribes and Pharisees, hypocrites …"

Without going into great detail, we can simply make the obvious point: Jesus was constantly being opposed by the "Bible-thumpers" of his day, meaning he was not one of them.

Why wasn't Jesus a Bible-thumper?

Why didn't Jesus use religious scriptures as a weapon to beat other people into submission? After all, he did refer to the Jewish scriptures in order to support his claim that he was the promised Messiah.

To me it is rather obvious that Jesus had two concerns for his ministry. One was to appeal to the Jews of his time and the other was to give more universal teachings that were relevant for people in other cultures and in another time. With that in mind, we can see that Jesus referred to the Jewish scriptures in order to make the Jews take a serious look at him and his teachings. It is obvious that Jesus came to bring renewal to the Jewish religion so why would he advocate a conservative or literal interpretation of the old scriptures?

Jesus respected the existing tradition, but not to the point where he wanted that tradition to be used as a weapon against renewal. This might cause us to question how Jesus looks at the way many Christian churches use the Bible today. Would Jesus actually want us to interpret the Bible literally or use it as an "infallible argument" against any form of renewal of the Christian religion? Would he want different Christian groups to run around hitting each other over the head with the Bible?

Would Jesus want Christians to fling Bible quotes at each other in a meaningless quest to prove some superior interpretation? This quest truly proves only one thing: If you are willing to use Bible quotes selectively, you can prove anything. Meaning that whatever you "prove" with one Bible quote, you can "disprove" with another quote. The overall effect of the quotation war being that both sides miss a deeper understanding of Jesus' teachings.

How would modern Christians treat Jesus?

We can be a bit more provocative by imagining what would happen if Jesus walked the earth today. Imagine that Jesus took on a physical body and walked the earth, giving spiritual teachings. If you consider why he might do this, one possibility is that he would want to give us an updated teaching. If the teaching he gave us 2,000 years ago is still all he wants us to have, why bother coming back?

If he did appear again, it is likely that he would give teachings that went beyond what he said the first time. How would Christian theologians and church leaders react to that? Would they even recognize Jesus? Or would they use the Christian scriptures – or rather their doctrines and interpretations – to argue that this simply could not be the real Jesus? Surely, they might say, the real Jesus would agree with their interpretations. How many modern Christians would do exactly the same thing to Jesus today that the scribes and Pharisees did to him 2,000 years ago? This leads us to a question that, in my experience, many Christians have never considered, even though it is both logical and important.

Why didn't Jesus write down his teachings?

As I have said before, you cannot say anything about Jesus without having someone disagree with you. There are indeed people who say that Jesus was illiterate. Even if that were true, he most certainly knew someone who could write. I think we can reasonably assume that Jesus was quite aware of how people can argue about anything. After all, he even had to deal with his own disciples arguing about who should be the leader after he was gone.

It shouldn't be all that difficult for Jesus to have foreseen that people would disagree about his teachings, which leads to the logical question: Why didn't Jesus have a complete gospel written down? Wouldn't that have settled the argument?

Well, actually it wouldn't. The Jews of his time had an official set of scriptures, yet there was widespread disagreement about how to interpret them. One of the more significant aspects of the Old Testament was the tradition of the prophets. In many cases a prophet appeared precisely when there was disagreement about the interpretation of scripture, and if the people recognized the prophet, he brought society forwards.

3 | Is the Bible Relevant to Modern People?

After some time, different interpretations again caused conflict between groups of Jews and another prophet appeared. Jesus himself claimed to be a link – possibly the last link – in this line of prophets.

What was Jesus' solution? According to his own words, he had not come to destroy the tradition of the law and the prophets but to fulfill it. How did he plan to do this? Again, here are his own words:

> And I will pray the Father, and he shall give you another Comforter that he may abide with you for ever; (John 14:16)

> But the Comforter, which is the Holy Ghost, whom the Father will send in my name, he shall teach you all things, and bring all things to your remembrance, whatsoever I have said unto you. (John 14:26)

Perhaps Jesus deliberately did not write down his teachings because he knew it would not prevent the emergence of differing interpretations. Instead, he intended to establish a tradition whereby people could receive ongoing instructions through direct intervention from the comforter, the Holy Spirit.

Jesus used the old scriptures only to point out that he was the promised Messiah. Beyond that he gave a new teaching that was more advanced than what was given by the earlier prophets. Apparently he intended to continue giving updated teachings by establishing a tradition where his followers would be open to the comforter. This means that instead of relying on (differing) interpretations of scriptures set in stone, the followers of Jesus could receive the living word directly from Jesus through the agency of the Holy Spirit.

How the comforter was lost

How did Christianity ever become a religion that relies exclusively on human interpretations of a scripture that was written down over 1,900 years ago and canonized over 1600 years ago? One of the most momentous events in this process was surely when the Christian religion became the official state religion of the Roman Empire. This happened when a struggling Roman emperor, named Constantine, decided to use Christianity in an attempt to unify his divided empire.

No sooner had Constantine stopped the persecution of Christians than he was confronted with the fact that Christians were bitterly divided into two groups. They were fighting over whether Jesus was a man like other men or whether he was God from the very beginning. This is what is known as the Aryan controversy, and it is one of the most significant events in the history of Christianity. So how come most modern Christians have never heard about it?

I am not going to go into details because the historical facts are well documented for those who are interested. My point is that the controversy culminated in the Council of Nicaea, which established the first official doctrine of the Roman Catholic Church in 325. This was a church council, but it was presided over by the emperor who obviously had the power to send Christians back to the status of being lunch meat for the lions in the circus. Constantine's goal was clear, and Constantine's goal was clearly political. He wanted to use Christianity to unify the Roman empire under one religion and one emperor. For that to happen, Christianity first had to be unified.

You will notice that at the time of the Council of Nicaea, the tradition of receiving direct guidance from the Holy Spirit had already been lost. If not, there would have been no need for the council, as Christians would not have been divided over the question about the divinity of Christ. The methods used by both sides in the time before the council truly are more like what you read about in gang warfare. They included beating up rival priests, disruptions of church services and even assassinations. It is clear that what happened in Nicaea was simply a typical human power struggle.

My conclusion is simple. Despite the fact that this might insult some Catholics, it is clear from the historical facts that the Council of Nicaea was not a spiritual process. It was a political power struggle. The result was a clearly political outcome where the stronger side simply trumped the weaker—and then the emperor enforced the result with military might.

The Council of Nicaea is often described as significant because it established the first uniform Christian doctrine. This was not a spiritual doctrine established through any form of divine intervention. It was a political doctrine established through the fist of a Roman emperor. It was the final nail in the coffin of any chance that Jesus' intent of giving us new revelation from the Holy Spirit would be recognized by the official church. Instead, the Council of Nicaea established a church that had now codified an official scripture and had started a tradition of defining official Christian doctrines. It very quickly led to the concept that anything which went beyond or contradicted official scriptures or doctrine would be labeled as heresy. It would then be "anathematized," which means cursed or banned.

In the year 325, we now have the establishment of an official church, which claimed to be the only true church representing Christ. It did exactly what the religious authorities of his time had done to Jesus. It elevated an already written scripture to the status of infallibility, it defined an official interpretation as the only true one, and it used this as a weapon against anyone who dared to reach beyond it.

Consider here that if the comforter had brought forth a new teaching that contradicted doctrine, then the comforter sent by God would have been labeled as a heretic. If you truly look at the tradition of the prophets, you can see the same mechanism. Why did God have to send a line of prophets to people during Old Testament times? Because after some time, some power elite had used religion as a means for controlling the people. God had to send another prophet in order to free the people from this elitist control. This also explains why the established elite often persecuted the Old Testament prophets and why an established elite had Jesus killed.

Only 300 years after Jesus gave his instructions about his followers being open to the comforter, the church that claimed to represent Jesus on earth had completely and hermetically sealed itself off from any intervention from said comforter. This leads to another logical question that most Christians have never asked themselves.

What kind of religion did Jesus want to start?

I will return to this question later, but for now I want to make a simple point. I am sure there are many opinions about which kind of religion Jesus *did* want to start, but perhaps we can reach a consensus on what kind of religion he did *not* want to start? Can we not agree that the last thing Jesus wanted was to establish a religion that was exactly like the Jewish religion whose leaders plotted his execution?

Let's be brutally honest here. There are Christian churches today where, if Jesus himself walked in there and made statements that contradicted official doctrine or a literal interpretation of the gospels, then he would he labeled as a heretic or as being "of the devil." This is exactly what the Jewish authorities did to him when Jesus contradicted their scriptures. *We have got to do better than that!*

How can we relate the Bible to our modern world?

As I talked about earlier, there are today millions of people who grew up in a Christian culture, but they have either abandoned Christianity or only go to church very rarely. If you talk to some of these people, you will quickly realize that many either have not read the Bible at all or they have read only the New Testament.

Many start reading the Bible with the best of intentions, but get stuck somewhere after Genesis. How can we in today's western world see any connection between our own lives and a God who told a tribe in the Middle East to kill all the men, women and children of a neighboring tribe? Are we supposed to think that the ultimate God encouraged genocide and took sides in tribal warfare on a planet that we know is like a speck of dust in an almost infinite universe?

My point is simple. Why don't modern people read the Bible? I think a big part of the answer is the way mainstream Christianity has been using the Bible, namely as a stick to beat us into accepting official doctrines even when they no longer make sense to us. I think another big reason is that it is becoming increasingly difficult to see the connection between our lives in the modern world and a scripture that was written down two millennia ago and has not been updated since. The word "Gospel" actually means "good news," but where is the news value? This leaves us with a couple of options. We can either give up on the Bible, or we can look for a different approach to religious scriptures. Perhaps the latter is the option that was most appealing to Jesus himself.

Jesus offered his disciples a form of
spirituality that was very far from
the image of spirituality created
by official Christianity.

4 | HOW DID JESUS TEACH HIS DISCIPLES?

People want an interactive form of spirituality

As mentioned, I have spent the last 36 years on a personal quest for a deeper understanding of the spiritual side of life. I have met thousands of people on a similar quest, and common to most of them is that they simply cannot be satisfied by a form of spirituality where they are passive recipients of what comes down from a class of priests or church fathers. In my experience, the modern people who have a love for spirituality need an interactive form of religion, a participatory form of spirituality. With that I don't mean that you are allowed to hold the tray of communion cups or sing in the choir. I mean something much deeper.

One of the big problems facing us today is that we tend to look back at history through a particular filter. When we look at the history of religion in the western world, we look through a filter, but we often overlook that the filter was created by the Christian religion. *The Christian religion itself has shaped how we look at the history of the Christian religion*. That makes it very difficult to see what official Christianity either cannot or will not see. Let us look at an example.

If you look back at history today, you might think that people have always taken the approach to spirituality that we see in official Christianity. What is that approach? It is based on the existence of one official church, which has a clearly top-down structure. There is an elite of popes, cardinals or bishops, and they are the ones who define what the members of that religion should believe or even what they are allowed to believe. The organizational structure and beliefs of the religion are defined from above, and all you can do as an "ordinary" member is to accept it or leave (but if you leave, you burn forever in hell).

In this context, the important point is not the outer organization but the spiritual content. What we see historically is that Christians are required to believe in a set of dogmas and doctrines that are defined by a superior authority. You either accept the doctrines or you leave the church—or at least keep quiet about it. There is little room for individual interpretation or even something beyond interpretation, namely individual confirmation based on experience. Is this the way it has always been?

I recently read a book by Karen Armstrong, named *A Case for God*. One of the things she describes is that for several centuries before Jesus' time, there were two distinct approaches to religion. One was what we see today, namely an authoritative form of religion, which requires acceptance of a priestly class and its definition of a set of beliefs. Besides this, there was a much more diversified form of religion that offered people a gradual path of initiation.

Through these so-called mystery religions, people were offered a step-by-step path whereby they came to grasp certain spiritual concepts through a direct inner experience. Instead of requiring people to accept outer doctrines on faith, this form of spirituality attempted to give people a direct, personal experience that was more than mere belief. It gave people an inner experience that for them confirmed spiritual concepts.

Again, if you look back at history through the Christian filter, you either know nothing about this form of spirituality or you think it was pagan, gnostic, heretical or of the devil. What if this was precisely the kind of spirituality that Jesus gave to his disciples?

Jesus promoted two forms of spirituality

Although I am aware that many people in today's world are turned off by Bible quoting, I think we can learn much from reading the scriptures with fresh eyes. After all, the scriptures – official and unofficial – represent virtually the only kind of historical evidence we have about Jesus. Here is an interesting quote that I mentioned earlier:

> 33 And with many such parables spake he the word unto them, as they were able to hear it.
> 34 But without a parable spake he not unto them: and when they were alone, he expounded all things to his disciples. (Mark, Chapter 4)

Look at the remark "as they were able to hear it." When I read between the lines, it is clear to me that Jesus gave teachings at two different levels. He had a more simple teaching for the population at large, and then he had a more advanced teaching for his closer disciples. The reason is that Jesus was aware that many people at the time were not ready for the deeper teaching, and he gave them a more simple version in the form of parables. Yet he obviously had much more to teach, and his disciples received a more advanced teaching.

How did Jesus teach his disciples? Did he stand on a pulpit and talk down to them by expounding on the existing scriptures—as we have all seen Christian ministers do? Or did Jesus teach them in a much more participatory and interactive way? What exactly did it mean to be a disciple of Jesus? Again, when we look back through the Christian filter, we might think it is pretty much like being a good Christian today.

If we read between the lines, it becomes clear that Jesus was a very demanding teacher. Being his direct disciple was not a matter of going to church on Sunday and then living a normal life the rest of the week. Being Jesus' disciple was an all-consuming experience. Jesus obviously did not teach only by talking to his disciples. He taught by his own example and by giving them direct experiences of a very different approach to spirituality than what you could find in the official Jewish religion.

What if Jesus offered his disciples a form of spirituality that was very far from the image of spirituality created by official Christianity? What if Jesus' inner form of spirituality was much more like that of the ancient mystery religions? What if orthodox Christianity has labeled this form of spirituality as heretical and has attempted to intimidate or scare people away from practicing it?

If we look at the historical facts without looking through the Christian filter, we see that after the Roman Catholic Church was formed, there were centuries during which any diverging form of spirituality was systematically and violently stamped out. If we look with brutal honesty, we see that official

4 | How Did Jesus Teach His Disciples?

Christianity actually stamped out exactly the form of spirituality that Jesus offered to his disciples. Does that really make any sense?

There is still a need for two forms of spirituality

I know some will say I sound very radical or critical. However, it is not my intent to say that official, orthodox or mainstream Christianity is wrong or should be abandoned. In recent decades, we have seen a rise in Christian fundamentalism, and the obvious reason is that there are still people in today's world who have a need for this form of spirituality. They need the sense of certainty that comes from believing that if they belong to the right church and follow certain outer rules, they are guaranteed to go to heaven. I have no issue with this, and I have no desire to argue against this approach to spirituality. I recognize that such people have very real needs and that their form of religion fulfills them.

What I am trying to point out is that there are also people who need a different form of spirituality. There are people who need a participatory form where they are given direct experiences that confirm the reality of spiritual concepts. It has been my experience that in today's world there are more people with this need than ever before.

The problem is that such people see no connection between their spiritual needs and Christianity. The reason is that 1600 years ago a group of Christian church fathers started a process that systematically removed almost all traces of this form of spirituality from Christianity. Jesus' own form of initiatic spirituality was removed from Christianity in a process that was politically motivated (more on this later).

Did Jesus want all of us to have his inner teachings?

Again, reach back to what Jesus said about the comforter. How could this possibly work? Was it only a small elite of priests or bishops who could receive this comforter? Nay, it seems to be something open to all on an individual basis. All people have the potential to receive a direct experience of the Holy Spirit, which will "bring all things to our remembrance" that Jesus wants us to know.

It seems to me that Jesus actually wanted to leave us with a process whereby anyone who was willing to follow a set of initiations, could receive direct, personal, inner guidance from the Holy Spirit. What would be the purpose? It would be that you can also experience what it was like to be a direct disciple of Jesus. Naturally, you cannot go back in history and physically walk with Jesus. But through the agency of the Holy Spirit, you can still have the experience of being initiated into the inner mysteries of Christ.

I think this form of spirituality could appeal to many of the people who grew up in a Christian culture, but who gave up on Jesus because they could not identify with the mainstream approach to spirituality. I think that if some Christian churches would open themselves up to this form of spirituality, they could fill the needs of many modern people. I realize that in the past many people needed someone else to solve their problems for them. In the modern age, most people need to be taught how to solve their own problems.

Did Jesus foresee what we experience today?

Is it possible that Jesus was well aware of the limitations of his time? Did he foresee that there would come a time when more people could receive his inner teachings? Take a fresh look at the following statement:

> I have yet many things to say unto you, but ye cannot bear them now. (John, 16:12)

Is it possible that Jesus taught the multitudes in parables because he knew that most people were not ready for his full teachings 2,000 years ago? Is it possible that Jesus foresaw that a time would come when many more people were ready for his full teachings? Is it possible that this time is *now?*

Here is the problem I personally have with mainstream Christianity. If we look at society as it was 2,000 years ago, we can see that it was very different from modern society. It is simply amazing how much progress we have made during these past 2,000 years, and I am not only talking about technological advances. The knowledge of the world that the average person has today is vastly beyond what the average person knew at Jesus' time. Is it not obvious that if Jesus had been on earth today, he would have taken advantage of this and he would have given us a much more advanced teaching than he could give so long ago? Beyond even outer knowledge, it is my observation that humankind at large has progressed to a higher level of consciousness than in the past. This means that many people in today's world can attain a much deeper understanding of spiritual concepts than was the case at Jesus' time. More people than ever are ready for the fullness of Jesus' teachings.

What Christianity is doing today is ignoring the obvious progress that humankind has made over the past 2,000 years. Instead of updating its message, it is still preaching largely the same message that was defined by church fathers during the time of the Roman empire.

Again, I have no issue with mainstream Christian churches doing what they are doing. As long as they still have members, they are obviously fulfilling the spiritual needs of some people. I think it is high time for a new approach to Christianity that can make Jesus and his true teachings relevant to the many people who have more mature spiritual needs. I don't think Jesus is obsolete. Yet I do think that the official image of Jesus is fast becoming obsolete for more and more people.

5 | HOW THE OFFICIAL JESUS WAS INVENTED

What did it take to be a follower of Jesus?

When we look back at the history of Christianity through the filter created by Christianity, we tend to think that the early followers of Jesus were pretty much like the Christians of today. When we think more deeply about this, we realize there were some substantial differences. As just one example, we have been brought up to see Christianity as a major, if not *the* major, religion. Back then, there was no such mental image in the collective awareness. There was no Christian religion with elaborate cathedrals, intricate rituals and clearly defined doctrines. There was only a single man walking around ancient Israel, giving teachings and performing certain unusual feats.

The early followers of Jesus did not follow him because they were brought up to believe in him. They were not brought up with the sense that Jesus had an authority sanctioned by the high and the mighty of their society. In fact, they had been brought up to see the Jewish religion as having that authority and as being the only true religion.

This means one very important thing: The early followers of Jesus were not in the mainstream, they did not need a stamp of authority. They were non-conformists.

Instead of accepting the claims made by the official religion, these people were willing to think for themselves. They were willing to defy the traditions of their families and society. They were willing to go within and find their personal confirmation through a direct inner experience.

The early followers of Jesus had a very different approach to religion than the approach most modern Christians have been spoon-fed since infancy. I have already mentioned the question: If modern Christians had been around at the time of Jesus, would they have recognized him as being a legitimate spiritual figure? The answer to that question depends on one simple consideration, namely whether people want to conform to the mainstream church of their time or whether they are willing to think outside the box. From the scriptures, anyone can read that Jesus was rejected by the people who wanted to stay within the confines of the official religion of their time. Many modern Christians – in their desire to conform to official Christianity – have adopted the exact same approach to religion as the people who rejected Jesus.

We now see that Jesus himself was a non-conformist and so were his early followers. Jesus was not the mainstream official savior that we have been brought up to know. Instead, Jesus was a radical preacher on the outskirts of religious life. As already mentioned, if the terminology had been in use back then, the leaders of the official religion would likely have labeled Jesus as a "dangerous New Age cult leader."

The reality is that Jesus was a spiritual revolutionary. It surely is one of the greatest ironies of history that this revolutionary teacher has been reinvented and turned into a tool for keeping people within the folds of the mainstream. Did Jesus

5 | How the Official Jesus Was Invented

really want his followers to become conformists? Are those who conform to today's official Christianity truly in line with Jesus' ideals? Or have they come to accept an image of Jesus that has little to do with the spiritual revolutionary he was? In order to answer those questions, let us take a brief look at how the official Jesus was invented.

Why we need to look at the history of Christianity

Even though I did not receive any formal religious upbringing, I had some knowledge of Jesus and a clear sense that he was a unique spiritual figure. I also had a deep intuitive sense that Jesus gave a teaching that was completely non-violent in nature. After all, he did tell us to turn the other cheek and he allowed himself to be persecuted and crucified.

I don't know if you have ever thought about this, but what happens to most of us during childhood is that we are exposed to various forms of trauma. Our families and societies tend to see this as simply "part of growing up." We are left to deal with this on our own—something we are ill-equipped to do as children. For me some of the major traumatic experiences during my childhood came when I either directly encountered human evil or learned about it in school or through books.

Some of the major traumas of my childhood came when I learned about the crusades, the Inquisition and the witch hunts. I intuitively knew that Jesus' message was entirely non-violent. I simply could not fathom how the very persons who claimed to represent Jesus on earth could kill and torture people, even their own members. How could people believe this was sanctioned by Jesus, even that they would be rewarded by Jesus for doing so?

I think this is a dark stain on the Christian religion, a stain that no major church has made a sincere effort to remove. You simply cannot remove a stain without openly looking at it and exposing the psychological mechanism behind it.

Just think about this for a moment. Here we have a Christian bishop who spends his day in a medieval torture chamber, seeking to get his own countrymen to confess to heresy so that their souls can be saved. In the process of doing this, he is willing to employ the torture instruments used at the time, including roasting people's feet over burning coals until their flesh literally began to melt. If people would not be "converted" by his gentle persuasion, he was ready to have them burned at the stake.

At the end of the day, he goes into the nearest church, kneels at the altar, looks up at the crucified Christ, and he is fully convinced that Jesus looks back with an approving glance. I am sorry, but unless we openly look at this and understand how human psychology can produce these kinds of contradictions, I simply can't see how we can free Christianity from its dark past.

I am assuming that in today's age, no one will call themselves a Christian and at the same time approve of medieval torture methods. Of course, not so long ago many people in Northern Ireland called themselves Christians and still approved of blowing up their own countrymen with car bombs. Even more recently, many people in the United States called themselves Christians, but they approved of their government launching a war in Iraq that caused the death of – conservatively speaking – 100,000 civilians. Some Christian ministers even claimed publicly that this was a just war and it was sanctioned by God and Christ. Perhaps I am simply being naive in expecting that Christians in general want to understand how we can free ourselves from this tendency to use religion to justify actions that our religion labels as sinful. Yet I assume there are some people who want to understand this, so let us take a closer look.

Jesus was a master psychologist

As I said, learning about Christian atrocities was a major trauma for me, and it helped set me on a quest to understand human evil. In understanding evil, many Christians resort to what they learn from the Bible, namely that demons or the devil himself can take over people's minds and cause them to do all kinds of things. This is what many modern Christian preachers use as an explanation, but interestingly the devil always takes over someone outside their own circle. Obviously, that can't explain how a medieval pope ordered the crusades or started the Inquisition, can it?

I am not here denying the existence of certain dark forces, but I would like to point out that the devil "out there" is in curious contradiction to one of Jesus' most pivotal statements:

> And why beholdest thou the mote that is in thy brother's eye, but considerest not the beam that is in thine own eye? (Matthew 7:3)

If we really want to understand human evil, we have to look at this very tendency to always point the finger away from ourselves. Obviously, Jesus was well aware of this psychological mechanism, yet because the general population at the time had little knowledge of human psychology, he had limited options for putting words on it and describing it in detail.

Here is a good example of how we can use the greater knowledge we have today to explain an aspect of Jesus' teachings that is very relevant to the spiritual needs of today's people. In today's world, some of the more progressive psychologists have given us a tool for explaining what Jesus pointed out. It can be summed up in one word: ego. By many progressive psychologists, self-help experts and spiritual teachers, the ego is seen as an artificial element in the human psyche. It has a number of characteristics, and chief among them is that it distorts the way we see everything. By "seeing" I don't mean our physical sight, but the way we "look" at life. The ego makes it seem real that we are separate beings, living in a world made of separate things and populated with other separate people. This causes us to feel threatened by those who are different, and it causes us to become self-centered, even self-absorbed.

The ego can be expressed in many different ways. Some are obvious, namely what we normally call selfish or egotistical behavior, such as stealing from others or killing people in anger or revenge. The ego can also be extremely subtle, and it has the ability to camouflage itself as being perfectly benign, even as working for God's cause.

You may never have thought about Jesus as a master psychologist, but it is not hard to see that Jesus had the ability to see through the smokescreens of the human ego. Once you begin to read Jesus' words with the ego in mind, you see how good he was at exposing it. Just take the situation where an angry mob is ready to stone a woman caught in adultery. Jesus makes one simple remark that exposes the ego so clearly that all members of the mob see it and go home.

Why the ego won't get you to heaven

One of the characteristics of the ego is hypocrisy. We believe we are oh-so good, but in reality we are being selfish without seeing it. We are putting on a facade in order to appear good, but underneath is a self-centered motive. Jesus often exposed this ego game in the scribes and Pharisees, and he actually made a remark that should be a stunning reminder of how good he was at seeing through the ego:

5 | How the Official Jesus Was Invented

> For I say unto you that except your righteousness shall exceed the righteousness of the scribes and Pharisees, ye shall in no case enter into the kingdom of heaven. (Matthew 5:20)

Could we perhaps reinterpret this statement to be referring to the hypocrisy that is a hallmark of the ego? The scribes and the Pharisees were doing all of the outer things right according to the law and tradition of the Jewish religion. They themselves were absolutely convinced that because of this observance of the outer rules and scriptures, they were guaranteed to go to heaven.

Jesus makes it stunningly clear that this kind of outer facade will fool neither him nor God. Even the many Christians today, who are following the outer rules and doctrines, simply will not enter heaven. We must do what the scribes and Pharisees were not willing to do, namely acquire true righteousness.

What does that mean? Could it mean that we must free ourselves from the human ego by letting that part of the psyche die in order to follow Christ into his kingdom? I will later talk more about the need to reevaluate Christianity in light of the human ego, but for now let us stay focused on how the official Jesus was invented.

Why was Jesus such a threat?

Once you begin to understand the human ego and how it works in subtle ways, you realize something profound. Traditional Christianity portrays us as mortal sinners, and scientific materialism portrays us as a kind of biological robots. In reality, we are psychological beings because everything we think, feel or do revolves around the psyche. You simply cannot under stand human behavior without understanding the psyche and its hidden mechanisms. As I have pointed out, Jesus himself was a master psychologist so how can we fully understand his teachings without understanding our own psyches?

If we truly want to understand human history, we need to look at how the ego has influenced major turning points, often setting society on a distinct course through the actions of a few individuals who were blinded by their egos. With this in mind, let us look at a question that few Christians bother to consider: "Who killed Christ?"

Most Christians believe the Romans were the ones who carried out the physical crucifixion, but that the leaders of the Jewish religion were the ones who started plotting Jesus' death. I see no point in disputing that, but now look at the psychological angle. Why did the Jewish leaders want to get rid of Jesus?

Just take a minute to evaluate the situation. The Jewish leaders claimed superior authority through the Jewish scriptures and tradition. They were on good standing with the Roman occupiers, and they no doubt had a deal so that if they kept the people quiet, the Romans would not touch the Jewish religion and its power structure. Why should these high and mighty people feel threatened by some fringe preacher running around?

Now take this one step further. Again, the official Christian filter has made us believe that Jesus was the only alternative preacher of his time. Historical research has revealed this to be very far from the truth. As mentioned, there were lots of people preaching a variety of beliefs, and the entire scene was reminiscent of the modern New Age movement. Jesus was just one among many preachers, which makes it odd that he was the one who was singled out and crucified. Why did the Jewish leaders even bother to have him killed? What was the psychological mechanism in these people that caused them to see Jesus as a threat that had to be eliminated?

Did the ego kill Christ?

Who – or rather: what – really killed Christ? Was it only those specific people, meaning that no other people would have killed Jesus? Or was it a general mechanism in the human psyche, meaning that all of us could potentially be Christ killers? For 2,000 years Christians have pointed the finger at the Jews, yet perhaps it is time we start looking for the beam in our own eyes? It just might explain the dark stains on Christian history.

As I said, the ego makes you feel like you are a separate being who is threatened by those who are too different. When you combine this with our survival instinct, you see a potentially lethal cocktail. We may see ourselves as good, God-fearing people who follow the Bible, and the Bible clearly tells us: "Thou shalt not kill." In reality, this is a totally unconditional statement. The ten commandments do not define conditions under which it becomes acceptable to kill. The ego is an expert at defining such conditions and making them seem valid and justified.

The ego is a kind of justification machine. It uses a selective type of logic in order to justify anything it wants. If the ego makes you think certain people are a threat, it is just a matter of how intense the threat seems before the ego can come up with a "perfectly justifiable" argument for killing those people. One argument is that some people are guilty of blasphemy and therefore are a threat to God's plan for saving the world. In that case, people blinded by their egos can justify almost any amount of killing—from one person to an entire tribe. Just look at how the ancient Israelites believed their God had justified the genocide of neighboring tribes. Do you think the real God took sides in what was nothing more than tribal warfare?

Here comes one of these questions you rarely hear from the pulpit: "What exactly is Christ?" Is it possible that Christ – in its most universal form – is what can empower us to escape the blindness of the human ego? Meaning that one of the main purposes of Jesus' mission was to show us that it is possible to transcend the ego-based consciousness and rise to a distinctly higher form of consciousness. This would mean that Jesus did not want Christianity to become just another religion that was influenced by the blindness of the ego and run by people blinded by their egos.

The ego versus the Holy Spirit

It is obvious that the ego was present in Christianity from the very beginning. We know this from the scriptures in the following passage:

> 33 And he came to Capernaum: and being in the house he asked them, What was it that ye disputed among yourselves by the way?
> 34 But they held their peace: for by the way they had disputed among themselves, who should be the greatest.
> 35 And he sat down, and called the twelve, and saith unto them, If any man desire to be first, the same shall be last of all, and servant of all. (Mark Chapter 9)

This struggle for supremacy among Jesus' own disciples is a very typical ego game. In a sense it should be no surprise that the disciples had egos—for if they were ego-free why would they need to follow Jesus?

5 | How the Official Jesus Was Invented

Our official Christian filter tends to make us believe that the early Christian movement was very homogenous and largely centered around what later became the official Christian church. Historical research, including the uncovering of Gnostic gospels, has disproved this assumption and shown a much more diversified picture. How could it be otherwise when Jesus did not set forth an official scripture?

During the first couple of centuries, the Christian movement – one could hardly call it a religion as we have come to see religion – was very diversified. There was no official church and not even an official scripture. Many separate groups had emerged, and their interpretations of the Christian experience were so different that they were often mutually exclusive.

This was a rather chaotic situation, but was it really that different from what Jesus himself had started? After all, he sent his apostles out to preach without a formal scripture or doctrine. He even told them to take no thought for what they would say because it would be given to them by the Holy Spirit.

Jesus did attempt to insert a unifying element into the early movement, namely the Holy Spirit. Does this necessarily mean that all people who preached by the Spirit would say the same thing? Is it not possible that when the apostles preached for different audiences with different preconceived beliefs, the Spirit itself would give a message adapted to the audience? An audience in Egypt might receive a somewhat different message compared to an audience in Rome.

After all, we do today have four different official gospels that have some clear differences, even incompatibilities. The official view is that all four were inspired by the Holy Spirit. Is this not logical enough when we consider the common consensus among scholars, namely that the four gospels were written for different audiences? Each gospel was adapted to the beliefs and culture of the intended audience.

My point is simple. Jesus obviously did not want to create the same kind of religion as the very religion that rejected and killed him. He did not want to create a religion with a centralized power structure, a religion that would be stifled by doctrines and endless discussions and interpretations of the letter of the law. He wanted a religion that was centered around the spirit of the law, a religion that was run by the Spirit and not by the human ego.

How a centralized church started forming

One of the main characteristics of the ego is that it feels constantly threatened. This sense of being threatened is difficult to live with, and if the threat seems severe enough, it is impossible to live with. The ego is in a constant struggle to minimize or remove what it sees as threats. The ego always points the finger outside ourselves, meaning our only option for minimizing a threat is to change other people. We are seeking to pull out the splinter in the eyes of other people rather than the beam in our own eye.

It now becomes clear that the kind of diversified and spirit-led movement which Jesus started will be a threat to those people who are blinded by the ego. We have already seen that the ego-blinded leaders of the Jewish religion rejected and killed Jesus, but why should we assume that there were no such people among early Christians?

Indeed, after just a couple of centuries, we do see the emergence of a movement that attempted to reign in the diversification in the Christian movement. There was a call for a unification of beliefs and doctrine, a unified power structure, unified rituals and, of course, a unified set of scriptures. Even so, there was still much diversity in the Christian movement, with new groups emerging and others disappearing. Could

5 | How the Official Jesus Was Invented

we not attribute this to the fact that people's spiritual needs changed over time? The Comforter sent by Jesus was perfectly capable of adapting the Christian message to the changing needs of the recipients.

As already mentioned, the movement towards a unified Christianity received a major boost when Constantine entered the stage. He wanted to use Christianity to unify the Roman empire, and that meant Christianity had to be unified. As mentioned, this led to the power struggle called the Aryan controversy, and if you read about it, you will see all of the characteristics of an ego-based struggle. "Good Christians" were willing to use violence, even kill, in order to exterminate what they saw as a threat to God's plan for saving the world.

In the following centuries, this development accelerated, and in several instances Roman emperors got involved. That is how Christianity was transformed from a diversified spiritual movement into a centralized religion that did exactly what the Jewish religion had done at the time of Jesus.

Among other things, this led to the concept that any idea which contradicted or went beyond official doctrine was heresy. The Church then started banning people who promoted such ideas by "anathematizing" them, which means that such people were cursed by the Church and presumably would go straight to hell. As we all know, this led to the banning and burning of countless books that contained teachings judged to be a threat to Christianity, including the works of the Greek philosophers.

Let me just point out a simple mechanism here. If you truly believe that you have a valid religion, which you have been given directly from God or Christ, why would you feel threatened by any contradictory idea? If you are convinced you have the truth, you simply preach your idea—which is exactly what Jesus did. Jesus did challenge the scribes and pharisees at the level of ideas, but he never resorted to violence or force against people.

My point being that Christ never used force whereas the ego will use force any time it feels the threat cannot be repelled in any other way. Let me say this more clearly: Any time people use force in the service of a good or spiritual cause, you can be absolutely sure that they are blinded by their egos.

Explaining the violent past of the Christian religion

As most of us know, the early development of a centralized Christian power structure led to countless acts of violence. Burning books is, of course, an act of violence, but still not in the same league as killing people. It is an undeniable historical fact that the Roman Catholic Church instituted many acts of violence, including the massacre of the Cathars, the Crusades, the persecution of early scientists, the Inquisition and the witch hunts. I know that those who want to destroy all religion love to exaggerate the figures of how man people were killed during this period. Yet even if we use the most conservative estimates, it is clear that thousands upon thousands of people were killed.

Given that these were violent times, there truly was much other violence in society. What makes the killings by Christians so shocking is that Jesus gave us a completely non-violent philosophy. Modern Christians do have an undeniable question to answer. How is it possible that the completely non-violent philosophy of Jesus was turned into a system that "justified" systematic eradication of entire groups of people, whose only "sin" was that they would not submit to Catholic authority?

Please don't misinterpret what I am saying here. I do not agree with the so-called new atheists who are seeking to eradicate all religion by making it seem like religion is the root of all evil. On the contrary, I would like to see Christianity be the

5 | How the Official Jesus Was Invented

kind of religion Jesus wanted it to be. Yet for that to happen, we need to look at Christianity's past and honestly ask ourselves how it is possible that the Christian religion could diverge so far from Christ's teachings that people started thinking it was justified to kill in Christ's name. How could this even happen?

As I have hinted at, I believe a big part of the explanation is the human ego. The ego makes people feel threatened and it gives them a never-ending desire to establish some state of ultimate safety and security. This causes people to build physical fortress walls, but it also causes all of us to build "walls" in our minds. One outcome of this tendency is to seek to establish some kind of system that is then raised up to the status of being ultimate, absolute and infallible.

If you take an honest look at the history of Christianity, is it really that difficult to see this mechanism at work? When the Roman Catholic Church was formed, Christianity simply became a tool for establishing what Roman emperors had dreamed of for centuries, namely an empire that could last forever because it could not be threatened by any power on earth. The rulers and citizens of that empire could feel secure behind their – literal and figurative – fortress walls.

There is a price to pay for this kind of "security" because it is truly what Jesus called a "house built on sand." Instead of being built upon the rock of Christ, the Roman Catholic Church was built on the power of man, which means it constantly felt threatened by the powers of man. If the Church had really been built on the rock of Christ, it would not have felt threatened, and it would not have used physical violence to defend itself against human threats. It would have done what Jesus did and have relied on the power of God, yet resigning itself to following the higher vision of God even if that meant its own physical demise. My conclusion is clear. If we truly want to rise above the – undeniably – violent past of the Christian religion, we need to use our modern knowledge of human psychology. We need to openly recognize that the Christian religion was influenced by the human ego and its need for security. We need to make a determined and intelligent effort to reevaluate every aspect of Christian history in order to expose how the ego caused Christianity to diverge from the course it was set upon by Jesus himself. If we continue to allow the ego to run its course, then it is not hard to prophesy that Christianity will continue its descent towards becoming obsolete.

Was the official Jesus invented by the ego?

Please be aware that I am not necessarily here trying to say that what happened in the past was completely wrong. A religion will only have followers if it meets their spiritual needs. In ages past, many people obviously did have a very strong need for physical and spiritual security. In today's age, I think fewer and fewer people have this need. Which means that a Christianity designed to meet the ego-based need for certainty and security simply will not appeal to most of today's people. This is another reason to reinvent Christianity based on the spiritual needs of modern people.

I believe that when future historians look back at our time, they will see that one of the significant trends in society was what we loosely call the self-help or self-improvement phenomenon. If you look at what is happening here, you see that the underlying psychological mechanism is that more and more people are beginning to take responsibility for themselves.

People are no longer accepting that their psyches are products of hereditary or environmental factors. They will not accept that their lives are locked on a track and that there is nothing they can do to improve their situation. Instead, they believe it is possible for each individual to take command over his or her psychology and actively do something to attain a higher level of consciousness, a level that is distinctly different from what we call normal human consciousness. The amazing thing is that this might be exactly what Jesus was teaching. Take another look at this famous quote:

> And why beholdest thou the mote that is in thy brother's eye, but considerest not the beam that is in thine own eye? (Matthew 7:3)

Isn't it possible that Jesus was trying to give a very profound message here, but that he was limited by the knowledge of psychology that people had at the time? What Jesus was truly saying was: "Stop trying to qualify for salvation by seeking to change other people. Start qualifying for salvation by changing yourself, by changing your own psyche."

What is it that needs to change in your psyche? Could it be that you need to rise to a level of consciousness that is distinctly higher than what we call normal human awareness? Might this be a state of consciousness in which you are not blinded by the human ego, but instead see with the clarity of the Christ mind? Certainly, Paul seems to have believed this was possible, as demonstrated in the following quote:

> Let this mind be in you, which was also in Christ Jesus. (Philippians 2:5)

When Jesus told us to remove the "beam that is in thine own eye," he might have been giving us a message that we are better equipped to implement with today's knowledge. "Thine own eye" is simply a symbol for your psyche, and the "beam" is a symbol for the ego. Jesus called us to follow a path whereby he will lead us beyond the blindness and selfishness of the human ego into the higher form of life of the Christ consciousness.

Based on my experience with meeting thousands of people seeking a new form of spirituality, I believe that the transformation of consciousness is a viable way to breach the gap that so many modern people see between themselves and Jesus. If Jesus was "reinvented," or rather rediscovered, as a teacher who gave us a systematic path for raising our consciousness, I think this Jesus would seem far more relevant to many modern people than the bleeding figure hanging on a cross in so many Christian churches.

In my observation, many modern people no longer need a savior who can do something for them. They need an example who can show them how to do something for themselves. Obviously, this is a thought that many Christian preachers will instantly label as being of the devil. Yet I will let these preachers continue to preach to their congregations, and in the coming chapters I will attempt to sketch exactly what kind of changes we must be willing to make in order to go backwards – or forwards – to a Jesus who can tell us how to remove the beam from our own eyes.

6 | NO MORE DANCING AROUND THE GOLDEN CALF

The religious supermarket

If you take a look at the Internet, it is clear that there has never been a time when so many and so many different forms of religion and spirituality have been offered to the public. It literally is a religious supermarket.

Imagine that people are walking down the isles and looking at the different offerings. They walk by a lot of shiny new products in modern packaging, and then they come to an entire isle labeled "Christianity." In this isle most of the packages have an old-fashioned design and many of them are covered in dust. Can you really blame them for moving on to merchandise that at least signals that it wants to appeal to modern people?

In today's world there are a lot of people who do have spiritual needs and who are open to some form of systematic or organized spirituality. These people are what we might call experienced or discerning shoppers, and there are some things you simply cannot sell to them. This leads us to a discussion of what Christianity will have to give up in order to have a broader appeal to today's spiritual people.

How Jesus became the only son of God

I still remember how I reacted when I was told that Jesus is God's *only* son. The first thought that popped into my mind was: "But then where did *I* come from?" I didn't mean that in an exclusive sense. I meant: "Where did all the rest of us come from?" If God created everything, then he must also have created me, right? And if God created me, how could I fail to be God's son? You might say this is child-like reasoning and while cute it isn't realistic. My answer is that Jesus told us that unless we become as little children, we cannot enter God's kingdom.

Now let us turn this around and ask: "Where did the idea that Jesus is God's *only* son come from?" Certainly, if you read the scriptures, you will find absolutely no place in them where Jesus – or anyone else – claims that he was God's *only* son.

The historical fact is that Jesus did not become God's only son until the Roman Catholic Church made him so. This started at the First Ecumenical Council in 325 when the Nicene Creed was formulated. After Christianity became the official religion of the Roman Empire in 380, another council in 381 updated the creed. The creed was the first "unified" definition of the basic beliefs of the Roman Catholic Church, which now started claiming that it was the official and only true Christian church.

The Nicene Creed says the following about Jesus: "one Lord Jesus Christ, the only begotten Son of God, begotten of his Father before all worlds, God of God, Light of Light, very God of very God, begotten, not made, being of one substance with the Father." Despite the obscure wording, the meaning is crystal clear: Jesus was God; *you* are not!

6 | No More Dancing around the Golden Calf

From Roman gods to a Roman Jesus

Why would the Roman church come up with this idea, given that the same church also formalized a set of official scriptures in which you do not find the concept that Jesus was the only son of God? They came up with it for a simple reason. The Roman church was created under the auspices of a Roman emperor who wanted a religion that could unite the empire under his reign. He wanted a religion that could effectively replace the old Roman religion.

If you look at the old Roman religion, you see one very clear characteristic. Its concept of "God" was rather similar to the story of a genie in a bottle. Most of the time, the genie is holed up in a bottle and thus stays out of your way. When you have a wish, you open the bottle and out pops the genie, ready to fulfill your wish. The Romans clearly looked at God as something that existed in order to do something for them, but which otherwise would let them live their lives as they pleased.

Another characteristic of the Roman religion was that it had many gods. There was a specialized god for just about anything you could want. The problem with this was that over time, people's faith in these many gods had weakened. This came from the fact that the Romans thought the way to get a god to do something for you was to make a sacrifice. The Romans obviously had a peculiar understanding of cause and effect. They thought their sacrifice was the cause, and the god doing something for them was the automatic effect. They thought they could buy their way to favors from the gods.

With this in mind, we can see why Jesus suddenly became God's *only* son, even "God of very God, begotten, not made." The Romans wanted a God who could do something for them, which meant this God had to have great power. Christianity was a monotheistic religion, meaning it had only one God. In order to sell this to the Romans, this God had to be more powerful than all of the separate gods together.

Christianity was also a religion focused on Jesus who had walked the earth like an ordinary man. How can you sell this to the Romans who are used to worshipping gods with supernatural powers? You have to make Jesus special so that he was not an ordinary man. He was actually God from the very beginning, but he had taken on the appearance of a man in order to descend to earth and do something for us that no ethereal god could do. Therefore, Jesus could do something for the Romans that the old gods could not do.

I still remember having an Aha experience while watching the old movie *Ben Hur*. There is a scene in it where Ben Hur's boyhood friend returns to Judea to become the new governor. He has a talk with the old governor who tells him about this new preacher (Jesus) who goes around preaching that there is divinity in every man. Whereupon the new governor exclaims: "That is ridiculous, we know there is divinity in only one man: the emperor."

We know that some Roman emperors had declared themselves to be god-like figures, but we also know the people stopped believing in this claim. With everything I have read about Constantine, it is clear to me that he was a practical realist. Is it possible he realized that as the belief in the old gods was waning, the claim that the emperor was God also had outlived its time? He had no problem allowing a certain branch of Christian leaders to elevate Jesus to this exclusive status.

Doesn't it seem rather peculiar that it was when Christianity became the Roman state religion that Jesus was officially elevated to the status of being the exclusive son of God—something he clearly never claimed for himself? Is it really so far-fetched that the Roman belief in the divinity of the emperor was transferred to Christianity and now gave exclusive divinity to Jesus?

The gap between Jesus and the rest of us

In my view, it is undeniable that with the formation of the Roman Catholic Church and the formulation of the Nicene Creed, a gap was created between Jesus and the rest of us. In fact, calling it a "gap" is a bit mild; it is more like an un-crossable chasm, a gaping abyss, a bottomless pit.

Again, one can take the view that this was a terrible mistake that forever set Christianity on the wrong track. Or one can see it as a practical reaction to a political situation where Christian leaders faced the choice between continuing to be entertainment in the circus or having a place at the seat of power. I don't really care how you argue the case because my purpose is different.

My purpose is to point out that while there may have been reasons for creating a gap between us and Jesus – and while those reasons may have been valid, or at least understandable, in 381 – they are no longer valid today. What may have made the Christian religion more appealing to 4th century Romans is one of the main things that makes it less appealing to people in the 21st century.

If you want to sell Jesus to modern spiritual people, don't present him as being fundamentally different from us. How can we see any connection between ourselves and this elevated Jesus? How can we see any connection between his teachings and our present situation? If we see no such connection, why would we believe Jesus can help us with our spiritual needs?

Another point is that today's spiritual people don't need the same kind of God as the ancient Romans. Obviously, there are still people today who want a genie in a bottle who pops out to do something for them and otherwise stays out of their way. Yet in the modern age, most people simply don't believe in a supernatural God who will fulfill their personal wishes. We are much more likely to accept a spiritual leader who shows us how we can use our God-given creative powers to do something for ourselves. As we will see later, this just might have been the kind of spiritual leader Jesus really was—when the Roman overlay is stripped away.

My conclusion is clear: If you want Jesus to appeal to modern spiritual people, don't set him apart. Give us a Jesus we can relate to, a Jesus who is more like us than he is different from us. Give us a Jesus who can do things that we can't do. Yet this is not because he was different from us from the very beginning. It is because he has walked further on the path of self-mastery, the path that we also have the potential to follow. Don't give me a Jesus who is like a genie in a bottle, give me a Jesus who is a way-shower—because he has walked a path that I too can follow.

Does Jesus agree that he is the only son?

I am not going to have a long discussion about this point because I think anyone who takes a neutral look at the issue will see the simple reality. I have already mentioned that there is no place in the scriptures where Jesus himself says he is God's only son. In most cases, Jesus presents himself as the "son of man." This is clearly done in order to establish a connection between himself and other people. Jesus goes out of his way to avoid setting himself apart from the rest of us.

When confronted by the scribes and Pharisees, Jesus does not deny that he is the son of God. Saying that Jesus is the son of God is a far cry from saying he is the *only* son of God. It is highly likely that Jesus would have reacted forcefully to the Nicene Creed. Just read the following passage:

> 17 And when he was gone forth into the way, there came one running, and kneeled to him, and asked him, Good Master, what shall I do that I may inherit eternal life?
> 18 And Jesus said unto him, Why callest thou me good? there is none good but one that is, God.
> (Matthew, Chapter 10)

What this man did seems rather innocent, but Jesus obviously used it to make the point that he does not want anyone to compare him to God. In other passages Jesus also demonstrates that he can "of his own self" do nothing, but that it is the power of God within him who is responsible for the works that are being done.

Imagine how Jesus would have looked upon being labeled as "God of very God, begotten, not made." He would likely have considered it blasphemy of the worst order. Has any modern church made a serious attempt to remove all influence of the Nicene Creed and its man-made elevation of Jesus?

Can we all become sons and daughters of God?

There are passages in which Jesus does not deny being the son of God. Yet even this might have a deeper meaning. I have already mentioned that Karen Armstrong has shown that at the time of Jesus – and until they were violently suppressed by the Roman Catholic Church – there were a great number of so-called "mystery religions."

A mystery religion portrayed life as a gradual path through which people were initiated into the mysteries of God. A novice was not able to fathom the deeper insights. By following a path of step-by-step initiations, people willing to apply themselves could gradually come to know the deeper mysteries. When this process was completed, the initiates had attained a higher state of consciousness than the average population. They were then endowed with the title: "Son of God" or "Daughter of God."

As we will see later, Jesus might have portrayed himself as such a mystery teacher. This means that he attempted to teach the mysteries by demonstrating them in his own life. The life of Jesus was meant to illustrate a path of initiation that is open to all of us. When we follow the way outlined by Jesus, we too can earn the title of being a son or daughter of God. Jesus at first presented himself as a "son of man" in order to demonstrate the process whereby anyone willing to follow the path of initiation can become a "son of God."

Do you think I am making this up? The person writing the Gospel of John didn't seem to think so:

> 11 He came unto his own, and his own received him not.
> 12 But as many as received him, to them gave he power to become the sons of God, even to them that believe on his name: (John, Chapter 11)

Paul didn't seem to think so either, as the following quotes demonstrate:

> For as many as are led by the Spirit of God, they are the sons of God. (Romans 8:14)

> That ye may be blameless and harmless, the sons of God, without rebuke, in the midst of a crooked and perverse nation, among whom ye shine as lights in the world; (Philippians 2:15)

6 | No More Dancing around the Golden Calf

> 3 Behold, what manner of love the Father hath bestowed upon us that we should be called the sons of God: therefore the world knoweth us not, because it knew him not.
> 2 Beloved, now are we the sons of God, and it doth not yet appear what we shall be: but we know that, when he shall appear, we shall be like him; for we shall see him as he is.
> 3 And every man that hath this hope in him purifieth himself, even as he is pure. (1John 3)

The last quote is especially telling. It clearly indicates that those who are willing to purify themselves as Jesus had done, shall be called the sons of God and shall be like Jesus when he appears. A Jesus who is a mystery teacher and demonstrated a path that all of us can follow will be a lot more appealing to today's spiritual people than the remote Jesus sitting up there at the right hand of God and who, although he has all power in heaven and on earth, apparently doesn't have anything to say to modern people.

The ego and the only son

Human beings are psychological beings. If we want to understand human psychology, we need to factor in the ego. How does the ego fit into this? The ego is constantly threatened, and it is seeking to compensate for this by creating the appearance of being safe, even of being saved in some ultimate sense.

At the same time, the ego has an insurmountable problem. Once again, we can see a hint of how Jesus might have attempted to explain to people – who had no understanding of the ego – how to overcome the ego. In the Gospel of John is an interesting passage where Jesus is trying to explain the keys to salvation to a man named Nicodemus. Jesus explains that we have to be reborn of water and of spirit. We might interpret this to mean that we have to go through a fundamental shift in consciousness, a change which causes us to transcend the ego. Jesus then says:

> And no man hath ascended up to heaven, but he that came down from heaven (John 3:13)

According to the definition of the ego used by many spiritual teachers today, there is a part of us that was created in a higher realm and then descended into embodiment on earth. The ego was not created in a higher realm; it is an element of our psyches that was created here on earth. When you put this together with Jesus' statement, you see what might be called the central problem of human existence.

What has happened to all of us is that we have forgotten who we truly are, namely spiritual beings who descended to earth from a higher realm. Instead, we have come to see ourselves and life through a filter created by the ego. The ego makes us believe we are separated from God and separated from God's kingdom—we are separate beings.

The problem is this: We know we have to be saved, but we think this means that we have to be saved as separate beings. What Jesus was saying to Nicodemus is that only that part of us which descend from heaven can ascend back. Meaning that the ego can never be saved. Because this thought is unbearable to people identified with the ego, the ego has to come up with an alternative view of salvation. According to this view, there has to be an external savior who does for us what the ego cannot do for itself.

The ego wants to elevate Jesus to a special status, and the more special Jesus is compared to us, the more likely it seems that Jesus can do for us what the ego cannot do for us. The ego has a clear tendency to turn a spiritual teacher into an idol and then worship that idol instead of the transcendent God.

Indeed, I will argue that the human ego – by elevating Jesus as the only son of God – has turned Jesus into an idol and has turned mainstream Christianity into a form of idolatry. Jesus would most likely have reacted to this with a stern rebuke. Of course, saying this leads on to the even more provocative question of whether Jesus saw himself as our savior, which I will talk about in the next chapter.

The virgin birth has to go

Before we move on, let us look at one more outcome of the idolatrous cult built around Jesus, namely the idea that he was born of a virgin. Clearly, this is another attempt to set Jesus apart from the rest of us by making him unique. Many Biblical scholars have pointed out that only two of the four gospels mention the virgin birth. Meaning that two of the gospel writers either knew nothing about it or considered it unimportant to their purpose for writing.

Many scholars also point out that the word "virgin" is actually a mistranslation of a Greek word that should more correctly be translated as "young girl," possibly as meaning a girl who was pure in a spiritual sense. Let us put this together with the existence of mystery religions that offered a path of initiation that was designed to raise people's consciousness. I find it very likely that Jesus' mother could have gone through a process that had purified her consciousness, which made her qualified to give birth to a child with a special mission. Yet that doesn't mean it was a virgin birth in a physical sense.

I know many Christians are very attached to seeing Jesus as special, and they will say it is degrading to question the virgin birth. I disagree because I believe Jesus was a very significant spiritual figure and as such the truth can never be degrading to him. I believe the real Jesus can stand up to any kind of scrutiny, and we do Jesus no service by upholding an image of him based on mistranslations and the ego's desire to raise up an idol.

I have no doubt that Jesus was conceived the same way as the rest of us, namely by our parents – as much as we might prefer not to think about it – having physical intercourse. I think acknowledging that Jesus was not born of a virgin only helps make him relevant to today's spiritual people. I also think Jesus went out of his way to avoid setting himself apart from the rest of us, and I think he would be appalled by the cult of idolatry built by official Christianity, including the claim of a virgin birth.

Having said that, I have no problem saying that the Spirit played a role in Jesus' conception. Clearly, Mary was much younger than Joseph and they were likely from very different family backgrounds. It seems Mary had entered a kind of religious order and had not planned to marry. I see no problem with both her and Joseph having spiritual or mystical experiences and encounters, which played a significant role in getting them to drastically change their lives in order to give birth to and raise Jesus. While this makes Jesus unusual, it does not make him exclusive. What could prevent the Spirit from playing a similar role in order to bring other children into the world?

7 | DID JESUS PREACH A PACIFYING FORM OF SALVATION?

Why do people believe Jesus promised an automatic salvation?

A few years ago, I was visiting a good friend in Los Angeles. A business associate of his, named David, stopped by my friend's office, and we ended up having a conversation about spiritual topics in general. It turned out David was the son of a fundamentalist Christian minister, but David was obviously more open-minded than most fundamentalist Christians. During the conversation, we touched on the topic of whether Jesus was going to do all the work for us or whether we had to do something ourselves in order to qualify for salvation. David mentioned the standard fundamentalist line, namely that all we have to do is to sincerely declare Jesus to be our Lord and Savior, and then we are guaranteed to be saved.

At that point, I spontaneously blurted out: "So are you saying that if Adolph Hitler on his deathbed had sincerely confessed Christ, Hitler would have gone to heaven?" A few seconds of stunned silence followed because obviously David had never considered this question. Then, he said: "Well, based on everything I was brought up to believe, I would have to say that he would." Yet from his tone of voice it was clear that David didn't really believe what he was saying. And quite frankly, how did we ever get to the point where millions of people actually believe this?

The United States is truly an amazing nation. A little over a century ago, several states were still largely wilderness, and now the U.S. is the largest economy in the world and one of the most technologically advanced nations. What drove this amazing transformation? A large part of it is the basic American mindset, which incorporates the deep belief that making an effort will make a difference, that hard work and individual initiative pays off.

Then how come America is the birthplace of Christian fundamentalism when fundamentalism is in direct opposition to the mindset that built America? Is there a more pacifying belief system than fundamentalism? All you have to do is to declare Jesus to be your Lord and Savior, and then your salvation is guaranteed. It doesn't matter who you are and what you have done, it doesn't matter whether you made an effort to improve yourself, and it doesn't matter whether your state of consciousness is high or low. All that matters is that you accept Christ, and then Christ simply has to accept *you*.

One of the cornerstones of Christian fundamentalism is a literal interpretation of the Bible. Try as I might, I simply don't see any place in the scriptures where Jesus promises that kind of guaranteed salvation. I don't even see any place that can be creatively interpreted to promise that kind of salvation. How did we get to this point?

Another dilemma faced by Christianity

A couple of years ago, I watched a television interview with Karen Armstrong. She made the very interesting observation that fundamentalism is a product of the modern scientific age. Fundamentalists take the scientific, rational mindset and apply it to scripture. I had never thought about that because fundamentalists are so opposed to science that one would think they had a very different mindset.

Karen Armstrong's point was that the scientific mindset has conditioned us to think there are factual, literal explanations for everything. Yet before the advent of the scientific age, people thought very differently. For example, before the advent of rational science, most people would interpret religious scriptures as a form of myth that could be understood and interpreted in many different ways. Most people knew that the scriptures – such as the creation account in Genesis – were not meant to be interpreted literally. Some were even open to the idea that a religious scripture could be interpreted at different levels of understanding, from basic to more advanced.

This got me thinking about where Christian fundamentalism came from, and it is clearly an offshoot of Lutheranism. When you look at Luther, you see two things. First, he lived in a time when life was heavily dominated by the Catholic Church. As I have already mentioned, the medieval Catholic Church clearly used power in a way that was incompatible with the teachings of Christ. It is very understandable that Luther saw the need for reform.

The second thing is that despite the fact that many Lutheran Christians want to idolize Luther, it is clear that he was a product of his time. You may have heard the saying: "History is written by the winners." For more than a thousand years, "the winners" were the Catholic Church leaders. They had blatantly rewritten the history of Christianity in order to prove one single point, namely that the Catholic Church was the only true representative of Christ on earth. My point is that Luther could only suggest reforms based on what he knew, and what he knew was very much shaped by the Catholic Church. For example, Luther simply did not have access to the knowledge about history and the alternative scriptures that we have today.

Although Luther correctly pointed out the need for reform and started the process, he simply did not have the knowledge to carry that reform as far as it needed to go. What has happened since Luther's time is that because Christianity has come under such pressure from scientific materialism, few modern Christian leaders have the willingness to carry that reform further, even though we today have a much better foundation for doing so.

Luther had the will but not the knowledge, and we have the knowledge but not the will. As I have tried to point out, without making the long overdue reforms, Christianity is a doomed religion. It is seeking to fulfill modern spiritual needs by using tools developed over a thousand years ago in a very different time—*and it just can't work.*

How did Jesus become a savior who does it all for us?

Let us take a closer look at Luther. He correctly saw that the Catholic Church had added certain elements to Christianity that had no scriptural support and contradicted the teachings of Jesus. One prominent example was the concept that you could buy yourself free from sins. Taken to its extreme, this idea took the form of letters of indulgence, which basically meant that you could pay the Church to avoid penance or punishment for sin. Luther clearly saw that this was simply a way for the Church to make money and expand its power.

You might never have thought about this, but Jesus obviously didn't own any property. Yet the very institution that claimed to be the only true representative of Christ was at one point the largest landowner in Europe. How did that happen? It happened in part because many people willed their land to the Church. Why did they do that, given that land was the only way for people to ensure the livelihood of their children? They did it because when death seemed near, they would call the Catholic priest. If people knew they had sinned, the priest might advise them that if they willed part of their land to the Church, their sins could be forgiven. When the alternative was an eternity of suffering in hell, that seemed like an attractive proposition.

Clearly, Luther was right that Christianity needed to rise above the idea that you can buy your salvation. Yet in seeking to do away with this mindset, Luther saw no other way than to do away with the concept of works. In reality, the idea of buying your salvation from the Church was simply an extreme interpretation of a much older concept, namely that in order to be saved, you needed both grace from above and works here below. You needed to make an effort in order to qualify for salvation. Where did this idea come from?

It actually came from the mists of antiquity because it has always been part of religious life. In many cases, it has been interpreted in rather creative ways. Let us look further back than Luther and what Luther knew about the history of Christianity.

As I have already mentioned, the Roman Catholic Church cannot be understood without focusing on the word "Roman." You cannot correctly understand the history of Christianity without looking at how this religion was influenced by the

Roman Empire. As mentioned, the Roman people at the time of Constantine clearly had the idea that a god is a being who can do something for you. In order to get a god to do something for you, *you* have to do something for the god. You are essentially making a deal with your god. For example, the Romans performed certain sacrifices, and this would essentially buy them favors from the gods—or so they thought.

The question is why people would actually believe this and why the leaders of a religion would encourage this belief? The answer is the human ego and its insatiable need for control. The ego has an inescapable insecurity, and it is constantly seeking to compensate for this by controlling its environment. At the same time, the ego prevents us from accepting full responsibility for ourselves.

We can all observe that life involves a certain amount of uncertainty. Even in the modern world, we cannot fully protect ourselves against mishaps, and this was a much more prominent problem in times past. What does the ego do in order to compensate for this fact of life? It creates the idea that whereas you don't have control over your life, everything that happens is controlled by one or several gods. If something good happens, you have found favor with the gods. If something bad happens, you have offended the gods.

This leads to the idea that if you can find a way to avoid offending God and at the same time get God's favor, you can still have some control over your life. Instead of directly controlling your life, you simply have to find a way to control God. This is precisely what is offered to you by the kind of religion that the Romans had when Constantine adopted Christianity as the new religion for his empire. It is no wonder that in the following centuries, Christianity became heavily influenced by this mindset.

7 | Did Jesus Preach a Pacifying Form of Salvation?

Of course, if we go even further back, we see that the Jews at Jesus' time also had the idea that they could control God. Their philosophy was that in order to avoid bad things happening in this world and in order to enter the next world, they had to attain freedom from sin. The way to buy your freedom from sin was to perform animal sacrifices in the Temple. Apparently, the supreme God of the Old Testament had a need for such sacrifices, and in return he would grant you favors.

Obviously, Jesus himself did not agree with animal sacrifices, and he sought to get the Jews to step up to a higher way to find freedom from sin. This caused Paul in particular to develop the idea that after Jesus' coming, animal sacrifices were no longer needed. Because the Jews were so attached to the belief that sins had to be washed clean through blood, Paul developed the idea that the spilling of Jesus' blood on the cross had been the supreme sacrifice. This had bought freedom from sin for all people so that animal sacrifice was no longer necessary.

I am quite aware that we can go into a never-ending discussion about many points here, but what I am trying to do is to stay with the big picture. The big picture is that the combination of the Jewish and Roman beliefs in sacrifice led to the development of a new religion. It said that Jesus was the savior and that he had saved us by paying for our sins through the spilling of his blood on the cross. Jesus had done something for us that we could never do for ourselves. Of course, in order to make it believable that a few drops of Jesus' blood could pay for all of the sins committed by humankind, Jesus had to be really, really special.

Why did people accept this? Partly because they were muscled into accepting it by the Roman power apparatus, and partly because the idea of an external savior is highly appealing to the ego. The ego loves the idea that by being a member of a superior religion and by living up to its relatively simple physical requirements, you have bought your way into heaven. The ego loves this because it knows that it can never gain entry into heaven through its own efforts.

If we want a Christianity that appeals to modern spiritual people, the entire idea of Jesus buying our freedom from sin through the spilling of his blood simply has to go. It is hopelessly outdated and belongs to a culture that is completely alien to the modern western mindset. Instead, give us a Jesus who shows us a systematic way to raise our consciousness whereby we transcend the ego-based consciousness that causes us to sin.

Why did the Roman leaders want a savior?

I earlier raised the question of why the leaders of a religion would promote the idea that you can buy your way into heaven by following the prescriptions of the outer religion. Isn't the answer obvious: It gives the leaders of that religion power over the people. If people believe there is a remote God in heaven, who is the ultimate power in the universe, and if the leaders of a religion on earth control access to this remote God, then those earthly leaders have absolute power over the people.

Jesus himself obviously didn't agree with this form of absolutist or totalitarian religion. The leaders of the Jewish religion had managed to make the people believe that only the priests had the power to absolve sin. If you did not obey the earthly leaders, your sins would not be forgiven and God would keep you out of paradise. If you did obey the earthly leaders, they had the power to make God open the door to paradise for you.

Why did the Jewish leaders want Jesus killed? Because he said that he and his disciples had the power to forgive sins, thus breaking the monopoly of the Jewish priesthood. If there is something people with absolute power don't like, it is when their monopoly on power is threatened.

Elitism in history

This brings us to another profound idea. History is written by the winners so who are the winners? In every society and every historical period, the winners have always been a small elite. I am not here talking about some world-wide conspiracy involving cloak-and-dagger secret meetings. I am simply pointing out that there is a universal tendency for a small elite to attempt to gain control over the general population. If we want to fully understand history, we need to understand this elitist tendency and the mindset behind it.

The elitist mindset is obviously an extreme outcome of the human ego. The ego seeks control, and the more people are blinded by their egos, the more control they need in order to feel secure. When we look at history, we see that the most totalitarian leaders have been the ones who were so consumed by the fear of their egos that they needed to have total control over other people.

In Jesus' own life, we can see how the attitude of the ego-blinded leaders of the Jewish religion and the Roman Empire contrasted the attitude of Jesus himself. Jesus was willing to lay down his life, and the members of the elite were willing to take life. Jesus gave us an example of a person who is free from ego and thus can give up his life for a greater cause.

How do ego-based leaders seek to gain control over the population? In any way possible. It is a brutal fact that controlling a large population through physical power alone is very difficult. The most efficient way to control a population is through a combination of physical power and ideas.

Obviously, any idea can be used to control people, but religion offers a very powerful tool for control.

Again, look at medieval Christianity. The general population lived in abject poverty and for them life was largely suffering. Why was it suffering? Because they were the virtual slaves of a small elite who lived very privileged lives, due to the fact that the people did most of the work for them. Why did the people accept this without revolting? In large part because their religion told them that their lives here on earth were not very important at all. What really mattered was what happened to them after this earthly life. Would they spend an eternity being tormented in a fiery hell, or would they spend eternity in heaven where they would enjoy the same privileged lives as the elite had here on earth?

What was the key to avoiding hell and getting into heaven? It was to obey the elite here on earth, the elite formed through an alliance between the secular and religious leaders. If you didn't revolt against the emperor and the power elite and if you obeyed the Pope and the bishops, you would go to heaven. If not ...

Various religions have found different ways to create this belief. In the case of Christianity, it took the form of turning Jesus into an almighty savior. He had suffered the way people did, and he had thereby bought their salvation with his own blood. Even though Jesus was clearly the savior, the key to receiving his salvation was still the outer church. Only good Catholics would be granted salvation by Jesus. The implicit claim being that while Jesus controlled salvation, the Catholic Church controlled access to Jesus. Thus, the Catholic Church controlled people as long as they were here on earth.

This power structure was possible only because of one thing: People believed that an earthly institution was the key to entering heaven. The problem is that Jesus didn't seem to be in agreement with this sentiment.

Is Christianity a religion?

Before we get to what Jesus actually preached, let me make a point that follows logically from our previous discussion. I have said that we today look at the history of Christianity through a filter created by that same Christianity. The problem is that according to this filter, Christianity has been portrayed as a religion. A religion is generally seen as an institution that relates to God, heaven and how we need to live here on earth in order to enter heaven.

When we look at the history of Christianity without looking through the Christian filter, we see that this is all camouflage. The Roman Catholic Church was never a religion. It was from its very inception a political apparatus, created for the purpose of controlling the population. It was designed to uphold an elitist society ruled by a small, privileged elite. Truly, I am not here trying to be critical towards the Catholic Church. I am simply looking at historical facts without interpreting them through the glossy overlay that mainstream Christianity has conditioned us to apply.

I have a lot of admiration for the Founding Fathers of America because I think they had an incredible awareness of timeless principles. One of the principles they wrote into the Constitution is the separation of church and state. In a historical context, this is a very recent idea because in most past societies, religion has been intricately entangled with the state. In most past civilizations religion served to uphold an elitist society that heavily suppressed the general population. In some societies there has been a rivalry between a religious power elite and a secular power elite, but in others there has been one elite controlling both the religious and secular aspects of society. Without the separation of church and state a democracy – which is by definition a non-elitist society – literally would not be possible.

With this in mind, we can take a fresh look at what Jesus actually preached because it seems pretty clear that Jesus was very much anti-elitist and anti-establishment.

Was Jesus a revolutionary?

For more than a century biblical scholars have applied something called the historical-critical method. The basic idea is that if we want to understand Jesus and the scriptures, we cannot look at them through the filter created by Christianity and our modern times. Instead, we need to consider the historical and cultural context. I do not see this as in any way denying that there are timeless elements of Jesus' teaching. I see it as a logical way to understand why the Christian religion took the form it took.

Let us try to mentally project ourselves back to the time and the society of Jesus. It is clear from Jesus' own words that the last three years of his life was a special mission aimed primarily at the Jewish people. We can assume that much of what Jesus did and said was shaped by the beliefs and culture of the Jews of the time. If we want to make Jesus relevant to today's non-Jewish people, we have to look at how the message was adapted to the Jewish mindset. We can then use that to extract the universal elements that apply to us today.

At the time, the Jews had a highly elitist society. Most people were poor, but there was a privileged elite, consisting of the secular and the religious leaders. The common people believed their overall concern in life was to qualify for entry into God's

7 | Did Jesus Preach a Pacifying Form of Salvation? 101

kingdom after their present lifetime. They were willing to accept a less than ideal life in this world in order to get a better life in the next world.

How would they qualify for this better life? There were two main elements. One was that they had to have their sins forgiven. As already mentioned, only the priests had the power to forgive sins. In order to be in good standing with the priests, you had to follow an elaborate set of rules that regulated almost every aspect of your life. Many Jews even today are very much tied to ritual and tradition.

The point is that an ordinary Jew of that time had very limited personal freedom because he was restricted by an elaborate set of rules. These rules made people subservient to the ruling elite while giving them the promise of a future entry into God's kingdom. These were the key ingredients:

- The most important goal in life was to enter God's kingdom.

- God's kingdom would come after this lifetime, not while you were here on earth.

- You could not enter the kingdom by your own power; you needed the religious elite in order to gain entry.

- You had to follow elaborate rules in order to gain entry, including animal sacrifices.

The image of salvation believed by the Jews was a pacifying image where the people could not save themselves through their internal abilities or power. They needed someone or something from outside themselves – they needed the elite

– in order to be saved. Suddenly, a wandering preacher, by the name of Jesus, appears in the midst of this highly regulated and ritualized society. He starts boldly preaching a form of salvation that is almost diametrically opposed to the official version. We, of course, have been so conditioned to look at Jesus' time through the Christian historical filter that we simply don't understand how radical Jesus' view of salvation seemed to his contemporaries. Let us take a look, and let us start with this remark:

> From that time Jesus began to preach, and to say, Repent: for the kingdom of heaven is at hand. (Matthew 4:17)

To us, there is nothing revolutionary about it, but to the Jewish leaders, this was like waving a red flag in front of a bull. Instead of the kingdom coming at some future time, which for most people meant beyond their lifetime, Jesus was saying that you can enter the kingdom right here, right now. This becomes even more provocative when we consider it in context with some of Jesus' other statements and actions.

Take the fact that the Jews believed following the outer rules and traditions was a fundamental requirement for entering the kingdom. One of these was the sabbath, which the Jews followed as religiously back then as many do today. If you have ever been in Israel on a Saturday, you will know that elevators run automatically so you don't have to push the button. Taking an elevator is not work, but pushing the button is work. When I visited Jerusalem in 2009, I got a very disapproving reaction when I unwittingly entered a Shabbat elevator along with some Jewish ladies. How did Jesus treat the sabbath? He healed a man on the sabbath, and he had no problem with his disciples plucking corn on a sabbath. When confronted by the

7 | Did Jesus Preach a Pacifying Form of Salvation?

scribes and Pharisees, he made a remark that must have been extremely provocative to them:

> And he said unto them, The sabbath was made for man, and not man for the sabbath: (Mark 2:27)

It didn't get any better when he continued:

> Therefore the Son of man is Lord also of the sabbath. (Mark 2:28)

You can begin to see why right-thinking Jews started dusting off the "blasphemy" word. Yet it didn't end there so let us take a look at one of Jesus' most revolutionary remarks:

> 20 And when he was demanded of the Pharisees, when the kingdom of God should come, he answered them and said, The kingdom of God cometh not with observation:
> 21 Neither shall they say, Lo here! or, lo there! for, behold, the kingdom of God is within you. (Luke, Chapter 17)

Again, with our filter, this remark seems rather innocent, and I have never heard a Christian preacher make any big deal about it. Yet I would venture to say that for the ruling elite, this is the most revolutionary remark of Jesus' ministry. If we don't understand the deeper meaning behind this remark, we can never make Jesus relevant to today's spiritual people. Nor can we understand his true teachings or qualify for the salvation Jesus offers us.

What was so revolutionary? Well, two things. One is that the Jews believed you qualified for salvation by following all of the outer rules of the Jewish religion. Jesus is openly declaring that all of this means nothing. No matter how religiously you follow the outer rules, that in itself will not get you to the kingdom.

The second part is even more provocative. What is Jesus actually saying when he states that the kingdom of God is within us? Is he not saying that if the kingdom is within us, then we don't need anything from outside ourselves in order to enter? We don't need an elite of priests to grant us entry, for the doorway to God's kingdom is located inside ourselves. We can enter it by using the faculties we already have. No external force controls these faculties, and thus no external force can actually control *us*.

If you believe the kingdom is somewhere outside yourself, it follows that there is a gap, distance or barrier between you and the kingdom. This makes it possible that some external power – be it a devil or an elite of priests – can insert themselves between you and the kingdom, making it seem like you can get to the kingdom only by going through them or that they can prevent you from entering.

Jesus was saying that in his view, this external salvation was completely false. Instead, the form of salvation preached by Jesus was an inner process. It was exclusively a matter between you and God with no earthly authority standing between you and the kingdom. Jesus was actually saying that the people did not need the power elite, and that is, of course, the last thing the elite wants to hear. The final straw then came when Jesus threatened their monopoly on forgiving sins:

> 22 And when he had said this, he breathed on them, and saith unto them, Receive ye the Holy Ghost:
> 23 Whose soever sins ye remit, they are remitted unto them; and whose soever sins ye retain, they are retained.
> (John, Chapter 20)

7 | Did Jesus Preach a Pacifying Form of Salvation?   105

This constituted a challenge so revolutionary that the power elite of Jewish society quickly had Jesus condemned to death and executed as a common criminal. They did this in order to make sure that no one would consider Jesus an authority figure who could challenge their own position.

As the conclusion of this chapter, it seems clear that Jesus did not actually preach an automatic or pacifying form of salvation. What kind of salvation *did* Jesus preach?

The driving force in the universe is light,
meaning that even our mental powers
are driven by light.

8 | DID JESUS TEACH INSTANT SALVATION?

Why do we need to be saved?

One effect of what I have called the mainstream Christian filter is that there are many things we tend to take for granted. For example, I rarely see Christian ministers or theologians discuss why we need to be saved. Of course, we have the standard line that we need to be saved because we are sinners, but when you think about it, there is a much deeper layer of questions to be asked. Just for starters: "Why are we sinners?"

According to the standard line, an almighty God created everything, therefore also creating our souls. Since God is supposedly almighty, he could have created us any way he wanted so why create us as sinners? Since God is supposedly good, why would he create us with a basic flaw that necessitated us being saved by having God's only Son – or rather himself, since Jesus is supposedly of the same substance as the Father – descend to earth and save us?

For those who have never questioned the standard Christian filter, these will be new and perplexing questions.

Yet for many of today's spiritual people, they are not new at all. In today's age, many people have thought very deeply about spiritual matters, and they have been willing to look beyond the standard Christian filter in order to find explanations that made sense.

Many of these people have been forced to look beyond the Christian religion in order to find such answers, and that is one reason they avoid Christianity. What I propose to do here is to take an untraditional look at what Jesus taught in order to see whether we can find answers between the lines. After all, we can assume that Jesus had answers to such questions. What did Jesus really say about salvation?

Who decides whether you will be saved?

Let us begin by looking at how we can be saved. As we have already touched upon, there are basically two views of salvation:

- **External salvation.** This is a process that involves fulfilling outer conditions, such as being a member of a particular religion, having sins forgiven, following a set of religious rules, having an outer savior take you to heaven, etcetera. The basic point being that you need something from outside yourself in order to be saved.

- **Internal salvation.** This involves changes that take place inside of you, meaning you do have the power to qualify for salvation. Take note that this does not mean your salvation is guaranteed or automatic. It means you must go through a process in order to qualify, but the process depends exclusively on your own choices—not on other people or a church. The main factor that determines whether you will be saved is your level of consciousness, something only *you* can change.

Take note of a more subtle aspect. The standard Christian model of salvation involves a very subtle contradiction, which many Christians feel but rarely verbalize. The contradiction is that on the one hand, the standard model does promise you a kind of automatic or guaranteed salvation. If you are a member of the one and only true Christian church and follow all of its requirements, you will supposedly be saved. The effect of this is that if you believe what Christianity says, your ego will feel secure and you can live in relative peace.

Many people find that at some point in their lives, they recognize a particular doubt about this scenario. The reason is that the standard model portrays salvation as a process that is decided by God—a God who is a mysterious being and thus his motives are unknown. You will recall that I earlier said all fear relates to the unknown.

According to the standard model, your salvation should be guaranteed by fulfilling the outer requirements, but you cannot really be sure. In the end, the decision is up to God or Jesus, and no one can be sure what they base their decisions upon. Why does the standard model contain this seeming contradiction and this definite uncertainty?

The standard Christian model of salvation was developed during the formation of the Roman Catholic Church, and the purpose of that church was to control the population. How do you control people? It is best done by combining a carrot and a stick. You give people a goal and tell them it is generally reachable, yet you want there to be an element of uncertainty as to whether the goal can be reached by them specifically. The effect is, of course, that people will remain obedient to the church and its leaders because they think their salvation depends on an arbitrary God whose favors can be secured by the leaders of the church.

When it comes to the internal salvation, the situation is different. There is no promise of a guaranteed salvation. It is not a matter of fulfilling outer requirements, and it is definitely not enough to be a member of a certain church. From a superficial perspective, it might seem as if this is a more uncertain form of salvation. In reality, the uncertainty is simply placed in a different location. In the external salvation, the decision as to whether you will be saved is made outside of you, meaning the element of uncertainty is beyond your control. In the internal scenario, the decision is up to you, meaning you can take control over your own destiny.

We already know which form of salvation most Christian churches preach. The question now becomes which form of salvation Jesus preached.

Did Jesus preach an inner salvation?

When you take a closer look at the external model for salvation, you see that it has a logical consequence. It portrays God as an arbitrary and conditional deity. God has essentially said that he does not want everyone to be saved. On the one hand, God has supposedly defined a set of strict conditions that we must fulfill in order to be saved. Yet in the end, God will decide whether you will be saved and there is no way for you to know what the decision is based upon. Essentially, God is an arbitrary, conditional being whose will can never be known. You will therefore always have the element of uncertainty that breeds fear. How did Jesus portray God? Take a look at the following remark:

> Fear not, little flock; for it is your Father's good pleasure to give you the kingdom. (Luke 12:32)

Jesus makes it clear that we need to have no fear. Why not? Because God is not an arbitrary being who wants some people to be saved and others to go to hell. According to Jesus, God clearly wants all of us to be saved. This means God must have made it possible for all of us to be saved.

What Jesus was really saying here is that God has decided that he wants all people to be saved. The decision as to whether *you* will be saved does not rest with God—his mind is already made up.

If the decision as to whether or not you will be saved does not rest with God, where does it rest? Where could it rest except with you? The form of salvation preached by Jesus was an internal salvation because you are the one who decides whether you will be saved. You are the one who has the power to make that decision. God wants to give you his kingdom, but he has given you the choice of whether you will accept or reject it.

Who can make you ready for salvation?

Yes, yes, I know some Christian ministers will immediately scream blasphemy, but I am not here saying that qualifying for the inner salvation is easy. Nor am I saying that you can just make a simple decision. Jesus made it clear that qualifying for salvation is no simple matter. In fact, Jesus' form of salvation is a lot more demanding than the form of salvation preached by mainstream Christianity. The internal salvation will always be more demanding than the external salvation.

What conditions do you have to fulfill in order to qualify for the kind of salvation Jesus preached? Let us begin by looking at one of the more baffling parables given by Jesus:

> 1 And Jesus answered and spake unto them again by parables, and said,
> 2 The kingdom of heaven is like unto a certain king, which made a marriage for his son,
> 3 And sent forth his servants to call them that were bidden to the wedding: and they would not come.
>
> 8 Then saith he to his servants, The wedding is ready, but they which were bidden were not worthy.
> 9 Go ye therefore into the highways, and as many as ye shall find, bid to the marriage.
> 10 So those servants went out into the highways, and gathered together all as many as they found, both bad and good: and the wedding was furnished with guests.
> 11 And when the king came in to see the guests, he saw there a man which had not on a wedding garment:
> 12 And he saith unto him, Friend, how camest thou in hither not having a wedding garment? And he was speechless.
> 13 Then said the king to the servants, Bind him hand and foot, and take him away, and cast him into outer darkness, there shall be weeping and gnashing of teeth.
> 14 For many are called, but few are chosen.
> (Matthew, Chapter 22)

This might seem to bring us right back to the arbitrary God who at first bids everyone enter but then throws out those who do not fulfill some mysterious requirement. We can resolve this by realizing that those who were bidden to the wedding were

8 | Did Jesus Teach Instant Salvation?

the Jews, most of whom ignored Jesus. The parable therefore makes it clear that Jesus had not come only for the Jews but to invite everyone who is willing to enter the kingdom. Again, we see that the major requirement is choices you make.

What exactly does it mean to wear a wedding garment? Let us remember that at Jesus' time people did not have the rational, literal mindset most of us have today. Jesus obviously was not talking about a physical garment. The wedding garment is a symbol, but what is it meant to symbolize? We can get a hint by looking at another parable in which Jesus uses the symbol of a wedding:

> 1 Then shall the kingdom of heaven be likened unto ten virgins, which took their lamps, and went forth to meet the bridegroom.
> 2 And five of them were wise, and five were foolish.
> 3 They that were foolish took their lamps, and took no oil with them:
> 4 But the wise took oil in their vessels with their lamps.
> 5 While the bridegroom tarried, they all slumbered and slept.
> 6 And at midnight there was a cry made, Behold, the bridegroom cometh; go ye out to meet him.
> 7 Then all those virgins arose, and trimmed their lamps.
> 8 And the foolish said unto the wise, Give us of your oil; for our lamps are gone out.
> 9 But the wise answered, saying, Not so; lest there be not enough for us and you: but go ye rather to them that sell, and buy for yourselves.
> 10 And while they went to buy, the bridegroom came; and they that were ready went in with him to the marriage: and the door was shut.

11 Afterward came also the other virgins, saying, Lord, Lord, open to us.
12 But he answered and said, Verily I say unto you, I know you not.
13 Watch therefore, for ye know neither the day nor the hour wherein the Son of man cometh.
(Matthew, Chapter 25)

What is the hidden symbolism? First of all, we have a reinforcement of what was said earlier, namely that the choice is up to us. Some chose to have their lamps trimmed while others chose not to. If we want to qualify for Jesus' form of salvation, we have to be ready, but the choice is obviously up to us. No one forced the unwise virgins to leave behind oil; it was their choice. What does the idea of trimmed lamps symbolize?

What do we know today that people didn't know 2,000 years ago? We know that, according to Einstein's theory of relativity, we live in a world where everything is made from energy, everything is made from light. The driving force in the universe is light, meaning that even our mental powers are driven by light. As you can see from searching a Bible, Jesus talked a lot about light. Is the concept of having your lamps trimmed a symbol for us radiating light from within ourselves? Jesus obviously wanted us to radiate light:

14 Ye are the light of the world. A city that is set on an hill cannot be hid.
15 Neither do men light a candle, and put it under a bushel, but on a candlestick; and it giveth light unto all that are in the house.
16 Let your light so shine before men that they may see your good works, and glorify your Father which is in heaven.
(Matthew, Chapter 5)

8 | Did Jesus Teach Instant Salvation?

Where does Jesus say this interior light will come from?
22 The light of the body is the eye: if therefore thine eye be single, thy whole body shall be full of light.
23 But if thine eye be evil, thy whole body shall be full of darkness. If therefore the light that is in thee be darkness, how great is that darkness! (Matthew, Chapter 6)

When we consider the hidden symbolism, is "the eye" truly the source of light, or is the eye a symbol for our inner vision, the way we mentally look at everything? Jesus came to offer us a fundamentally different way to look at life than what is normal for most people. In order to have our lamps trimmed and put on the wedding garment, we have to go through an interior change, a shift in consciousness.

As mentioned before, Jesus made it clear that the kingdom of God does not come by observing the outer rules and doctrines of a religion on earth. He even said that we will never find the kingdom as long as we are looking for it outside ourselves. If we truly want to find the kingdom, we have to look for it in a very specific place: "For behold, the kingdom of God is within you." What is within us?

Are we to interpret this literally and say the kingdom is not located "up there" in heaven but that there is an actual kingdom of God inside of us? Obviously, with our modern knowledge, we know this cannot be what Jesus meant. What do we know today that people did not know 2,000 years ago? We know a lot more about the human psyche than people did back then. Is it not reasonable to assume that the kingdom that is within us is the mind or psyche, meaning that the key to finding the kingdom of God is found in the psyche?

We can now make a conclusion that shakes the very foundations of the Christian model of salvation. According to Jesus, the key to salvation is to change our state of consciousness!

Salvation is not a matter of living up to external conditions, as the scribes and the Pharisees claimed. Jesus made it clear that if we want to be saved, we had better find a higher form of righteousness than that claimed by these hypocrites. In order to qualify for the salvation that Jesus preached, we have to go through a dramatic and fundamental shift in consciousness. How dramatic is the shift required? As dramatic as we can possibly imagine: as the difference between life and death.

Did Jesus say most people are dead?

I am well aware that what I am saying here is a severe challenge to the view of salvation that has been presented by official Christianity for at least 1,600 years. As you might have started to realize, I don't really care what official Christianity says because my primary concern is what Jesus says. I don't want some watered-down version that was distorted by ancient political power-plays. I want the pure truth that Jesus wanted me to have. Let us take another look beyond the standard model of salvation.

There is a very mysterious passage, and I have yet to find a Christian minister who can explain it in a way that makes sense to me. Let me give it to you without any further introduction:

> 57 And it came to pass that, as they went in the way, a certain man said unto him, Lord, I will follow thee whithersoever thou goest.
> 58 And Jesus said unto him, Foxes have holes, and birds of the air have nests; but the Son of man hath not where to lay his head.
> 59 And he said unto another, Follow me. But he said, Lord, suffer me first to go and bury my father.

8 | Did Jesus Teach Instant Salvation?

> 60 Jesus said unto him, Let the dead bury their dead: but go thou and preach the kingdom of God.
> 61 And another also said, Lord, I will follow thee; but let me first go bid them farewell, which are at home at my house.
> 62 And Jesus said unto him, No man, having put his hand to the plough, and looking back, is fit for the kingdom of God. (Luke, Chapter 9)

Let us take a closer look at the situation. Jesus tells one man to follow him, but the man says that his father has just died and he wants to first go to the funeral. Jesus' rather baffling answer is: "Let the dead bury their dead." What on earth are we to make of a remark like that?

When we put it together with what we have discussed above, we can begin to make sense of it. Obviously, the man Jesus is talking to is what we would call alive and so are the family and friends of his father. Corpses obviously don't run around burying other corpses so what Jesus is talking about here is not a distinction between being physically alive and physically dead. The only logical conclusion is that Jesus used the words "alive" and "dead" as a symbol for something else.

If it is true that Jesus preached a form of salvation that depends on our state of consciousness, we can gain a higher perspective. It seems that according to Jesus, there are two fundamentally different states of consciousness available to human beings. How different are they? The most common state is what Jesus considers a form of being physically alive but spiritually dead. The other is where we are both physically and spiritually alive.

We now see the possibility that in order to qualify for Jesus' form of salvation, we have to go through a fundamental shift in consciousness so we move from being spiritually dead to being spiritually alive. A rather stunning contrast to the standard Christian model, but also a perspective that is a lot more appealing to many of today's spiritual people.

First of all, it is not a pacifying form of salvation. It does not depend on an external church, something that will appeal to many modern people. Secondly, it is very much in line with the modern mindset in which the world can be understood in terms of cause and effect.

Let me return to my previous question of why we need to be saved. We can now see that according to Jesus, the effect (that we need to be saved) has a hidden cause, namely that we have descended into a lower state of consciousness in which we are dead in a spiritual sense. Once we understand this state of consciousness and what caused us to descend into it, we will also understand how we can raise ourselves out of it by trimming our lamps and putting on the wedding garment.

9 | WHAT KIND OF TEACHER WAS JESUS?

What was the purpose of Jesus' teaching?

I know many Christians are extremely attached to having Jesus be the savior, and they tend to react aggressively when you talk about Jesus being "only" a teacher. Yet I am not saying Jesus wasn't more than a teacher; I am simply saying that he was also a teacher. Anyone who has ever read the New Testament will know that Jesus obviously spent a lot of time teaching. If you really need it, here is just one quote:

> And Jesus went about all Galilee, teaching in their synagogues, and preaching the gospel of the kingdom, and healing all manner of sickness and all manner of disease among the people. (Matthew 4:23)

Let us just stay with that thought for a moment. Let us again look at the typical fundamentalist claim, namely that all you need in order to be saved is to declare Jesus to be your Lord and Savior. If that is true, why did Jesus bother going around teaching people? Why not simply go around telling them to accept him as their Lord and Savior, if that really was the only requirement?

Why does a teacher teach? The standard view we have today is that a teacher gives knowledge to the students. Obviously, you can say Jesus did this, but there seems to have been another purpose for Jesus' teaching. Jesus was constantly being attacked by the scribes, the Pharisees and the lawyers, and these people were more like the modern concept of a teacher. They taught in an intellectual, linear, analytical way.

How did Jesus interact with these people? He clearly did not go into an intellectual or analytical discussion with them. Instead, he attempted to confound their intellectual arguments, almost like a Zen master who seeks to neutralize the linear mind with a Koan, a riddle that cannot be understood intellectually. As just one example, take the incident where the scribes and Pharisees accuse Jesus because his disciples plucked corn on the sabbath. His koan-like answer is: "The sabbath was made for man, not man for the sabbath." Here are a couple of other examples that indicate Jesus had a unique way of teaching:

> And they were astonished at his doctrine: for he taught them as one that had authority, and not as the scribes. (Mark 1:22)

> And the scribes and chief priests heard it, and sought how they might destroy him: for they feared him, because all the people was astonished at his doctrine. (Mark 11:18)

The conclusion we can make is that when Jesus taught, it was not in order to give people intellectual knowledge. He did not want his followers to sit around and have intellectual discussions with the scribes and Pharisees. What did he want from his followers? When we keep in mind what we discussed in the last chapter, is it not obvious that the real goal of Jesus' teaching was to help people go through the fundamental shift in consciousness that is the key requirement for salvation?

How did Jesus want us to get knowledge?

What could facilitate such a shift in consciousness? How did Jesus want us to acquire knowledge? Take a look at the following quote:

> Woe unto you, lawyers! for ye have taken away the key of knowledge: ye entered not in yourselves, and them that were entering in ye hindered. (Luke 11:52)

I have never heard a Christian minister try to explain what this mysterious "key of knowledge" might be. One thing is clear: Jesus thought the lawyers – meaning the elite of the Jewish religion – had taken it away from the people. Why would an elite want to take anything away from the people? Could it be in order to control them? This means that when people use the key of knowledge, they cannot be controlled.

Where do we gain access to the key of knowledge? Perhaps we can find it the same place Jesus said we find the kingdom of God: inside our own minds? Jesus did not want us to have outer, intellectual knowledge of his teachings; he wanted us to have a deeper form of knowledge, which we today would call intuitive or experiential knowledge. He did not want us to simply understand his teachings intellectually; he wanted us to experience their deeper reality.

How do you attain this deeper experience? As already mentioned, giving people this deeper experience of spiritual concepts is precisely the aim of the mystery religions. They take people on a gradual path that enables them to gain a deeper experience of spiritual concepts. This is what many groups among the early Christians called "gnosis." The deeper meaning is that you do not attain knowledge as a subject studying a separate object. Instead, you break down the subject-object barrier and attain oneness, gnosis, with the object.

Obviously, the Roman Catholic Church made this form of knowledge anathema, saying we are only allowed to know what the priests tell us. The lawyers of the Christian religion have done exactly the same thing as the lawyers of the Jewish religion. Do you really think Jesus approves of this?

In my view, Jesus was well aware that the human mind has a built-in capacity for attaining a higher form of knowledge. While Jesus realized the general population was not ready for it, he attempted to teach it to his closer followers. It is precisely this "key of knowledge" that gives all of us the potential to attune our minds to Jesus' comforter whereby we can all know the true, inner teachings of Jesus. I believe that in our time many more people are ready to activate this inherent ability of our minds.

Once again, we see that Jesus was anti-elitist. According to any mainstream religion, only an elite of religious leaders can correctly interpret scripture or attain valid knowledge. According to Jesus, every human being has the potential to develop this ability. The use of this ability is not a product of holding a position in an earthly church. It is exclusively a product of your state of consciousness. Again, the choice to raise your state of consciousness is entirely up to you.

Has Christianity degraded Jesus as a teacher?

Have you ever considered the hidden meaning behind the remark that Jesus "taught them as one that had authority?" We can now see a rather interesting possibility.

Obviously, the standard Christian model says that Jesus taught with authority because he did have authority, given that he was God's only son—or "God of very god." We now see a different possibility. Jesus taught that the key to salvation is to go through a fundamental shift in consciousness. The reason he taught with authority is that he himself had already gone through that shift.

Jesus had walked the path he was teaching to others; he had found and applied the key of knowledge. He had broken down the subject-object barrier between himself and God and attained gnosis with God, as witnessed in his statement: "I and my Father are one." Jesus was teaching with authority and not as the scribes because they were teaching something they only understood intellectually. Jesus had lived and experienced it, and that is why he taught with the authority that comes from direct experience.

This is an idea that is completely blasphemous to a mainstream Christian, but why is it blasphemous? If you absolutely want Jesus to be different from the rest of us, you will have to say that the indication that Jesus was not perfect, but had to walk a gradual path, degrades his divinity. My response to that will be that I think the standard model is what is degrading to Jesus. He obviously came to teach, but by setting him apart from the rest of us in a fundamental way, mainstream Christianity has degraded Jesus as a teacher. By elevating him to the status of being so different from us, Christianity has made it almost impossible for Jesus to reach his goal for teaching. The reason being that the rest of us can't relate to him, and that is why more and more people in the modern world ignore Jesus altogether.

Who is the most effective teacher? Is it one standing high above us on a pedestal where he is unreachable? Or is it one we can relate to because we can see he knows what we are going through, and we can see he has demonstrated the path he is teaching. I think the most effective teacher is the one who teaches by example.

Did Jesus have a learning curve?

Of course, here we once again run into the mainstream claim that Jesus must be special. One outcome of this is that Jesus was special before he was even born. Not only was he born of a virgin, but it is commonly assumed that Jesus was born in a state of perfection. Supposedly, he did not have to go through a gradual path of learning in order to qualify for his mission. Is that claim realistic?

You may be aware that there are people who dispute that Jesus actually existed as a historical person. The reason for this is somewhat understandable because we do have very little historical evidence for his existence. The main evidence we have is the four gospels, and even they are clearly not historical documents since they do not give much biographical information about Jesus' life. They are focused on his three-year mission in ancient Israel.

If you look at how the gospels describe Jesus' life, you see at least one peculiarity. Two of the gospels mention his birth whereas the two others don't mention it at all. Then we pretty much jump to the point where Jesus begins his public mission, which presumably happens at the age of 30. What did Jesus do with himself for those 30 years? The only thing we know is an incident that happened at the age of 12 when his parents had taken him to Jerusalem. At one point they become aware that Jesus is missing, and after a frantic search, they find him in the temple:

> 46 And it came to pass that after three days they found him in the temple, sitting in the midst of the doctors, both hearing them, and asking them questions.
> 47 And all that heard him were astonished at his understanding and answers.
> 48 And when they saw him, they were amazed: and his mother said unto him, Son, why hast thou thus dealt with us? behold, thy father and I have sought thee sorrowing.
> 49 And he said unto them, How is it that ye sought me? wist ye not that I must be about my Father's business?
> 50 And they understood not the saying which he spake unto them. (Luke, Chapter 2)

This is a rather astonishing passage and for several reasons. The key remark is, of course, the words: "wist ye not that I must be about my Father's business?" They indicate that at the age of 12, Jesus had a clear vision that he had a particular mission in life. Might this mean that Jesus knew he had to educate himself in order to qualify for his mission? Why else would he be "hearing" the doctors and asking them questions?

What we see from his parent's reaction is that they did not understand what he meant with "my Father's business." This reaction is the best argument against the standard view of Jesus' life, namely that between 12 and 30 he was an apprentice in his father's carpenter's shop in Nazareth. Clearly, if Jesus says that he must be about his father's business, and if Joseph does not understand what he means, then Jesus was not talking about being a carpenter with his physical father. He was talking about the business of his spiritual father.

What was the business of Jesus' spiritual father? Part of it was to teach people how to go through a fundamental shift in consciousness. This makes it necessary for us to consider a rather unusual question.

Do Christians think God is stupid?

We have established that part of Jesus' mission was to teach. We can reason that God sent Jesus to earth partly to teach us something. That something relates to us going through a shift in consciousness. If God wants us to get this lesson, and if God is not stupid, does it not stand to reason that God would send us a teacher who had the best possible qualifications for teaching us this lesson?

If we are to learn the lesson of how to transform our state of consciousness, how can this happen? Can we change our consciousness in one dramatic event, or is it more likely that we will have to follow a gradual path? Obviously, the latter is the more likely scenario for most of us.

If Jesus came to teach us a gradual path that leads to a higher state of consciousness, does it not stand to reason that in order to be the best possible teacher for us, he himself would have followed the same path that he knew he was going to teach to others? As far as I am concerned, people can still believe that Jesus was special from the very beginning. We can say that Jesus actually didn't need to follow the path in order for him to grow in consciousness, but he only followed the path in order to demonstrate it.

Either way, my point is that it seems likely that between the ages of 12 and 30, Jesus went on a personal quest for teachers and teachings that could help him go through a gradual process of raising his consciousness. After all, it is pretty clear that even if Jesus himself was perfect from the beginning, the rest of us are not. If you really are perfect and never had to learn how to raise your consciousness, how can you teach others to do this? Are you not a far better teacher if you know the difficulties your students are facing in their own minds?

Did Jesus follow a personal quest?

If you look at history through the standard Christian filter, you would think the religious life of the ancient world was very simple. If you lived in ancient Israel, you were either a mainstream Jew or you followed Jesus. As mentioned before, the reality was very different with a large number of religious groups and teachers. One example from Israel itself was the Essenes, and there is historical evidence that Jesus had some involvement with the Essene community at Qumran (where the Dead Sea scrolls were found).

Another component of the religious landscape was the so-called mystery religions. As mentioned, they clearly taught a gradual path of initiation, which was directly aimed at producing a dramatic shift in consciousness. Of course, ancient Israel had quite a trade with "the East," which inevitably would have exchanged not only goods but also ideas. In India there is a very old tradition of spiritual teachers taking students on a gradual path towards a higher state of consciousness. It is entirely possible that Jesus could have been exposed to this initiatic approach to spirituality.

If we are willing to read between the lines, we can consider why three "wise men" bothered to travel all the way from "the East" in order to pay homage to the infant Jesus. Is it possible that they were spiritual teachers and that they left an offer to teach Jesus when he was old enough? We know Jesus had an uncle, named Joseph of Aramithea, who supposedly did trade with the East. Is it not impossible that the teen-age Jesus would have followed one of his uncle's caravans in search of a spiritual teacher?

Several independent sources claim there are historical records showing that a young Jesus did travel in the East and even gained some fame as a spiritual teacher and miracle worker. Is it not logical that if Jesus at the age of 12 knew he had a spiritual mission, which would not begin until later in life, he would have set out on a personal quest to make himself ready for that mission?

If part of his mission was to be a spiritual teacher, does it not seem logical that Jesus would familiarize himself with a variety of the teachings that were available at the time? Does it not seem logical he would walk the path that he would later teach to others? To me this is far more logical than having Jesus be a carpenter's helper in Nazareth for 17 years, and then suddenly waking up one morning, saying: "Oh, now it's time to be the Messiah; see you, Dad."

Was Jesus ready for his mission from birth?

Aside from going on a personal quest in order to prepare for his mission, did Jesus actually need other people to help him get ready for his mission? According to the gospels, John the Baptist might indeed have served as a teacher or initiator for Jesus. Why did Jesus go to John in order to be baptized? Is it possible Jesus saw this as an initiation that was the culmination of the process of preparing for his mission? It was when he was baptized by John that he saw the Holy Spirit descend and heard God speak to him.

This clearly indicates that Jesus was not born fully ready for his mission, but had to go through a gradual path of making himself ready. We can all relate to Jesus in a much more personal way because we now realize that Jesus himself followed the path that we all have the potential to follow. Of course, it is also possible that Jesus only followed the path in order to teach us. Look at this passage:

> 13 Then cometh Jesus from Galilee to Jordan unto John, to be baptized of him.
> 14 But John forbad him, saying, I have need to be baptized of thee, and comest thou to me?
> 15 And Jesus answering said unto him, Suffer it to be so now: for thus it becometh us to fulfil all righteousness. Then he suffered him.
> 16 And Jesus, when he was baptized, went up straightway out of the water: and, lo, the heavens were opened unto him, and he saw the Spirit of God descending like a dove, and lighting upon him:
> 17 And lo a voice from heaven, saying, This is my beloved Son, in whom I am well pleased. (Matthew, Chapter 3)

It seems that John says he is not worthy to initiate Jesus. Yet Jesus insists on going through the ritual, and then he does have a genuine spiritual and mystical experience as a result. This might indicate that even if Jesus did not strictly need to be initiated by John, he did it in order to demonstrate the path to the rest of us—the path of initiation under a spiritual teacher.

It is also interesting that after this experience – in which Jesus moves a dramatic step closer to starting his mission – he is still not quite ready. The spirit leads him into the wilderness where he first fasts for a long time before he has to face one more initiation, namely to be tempted by the devil.

Again, you can take two approaches to this. One is that Jesus was following a gradual path of initiation and that he needed to face and pass this test in order to be ready for his mission. The other is that Jesus might not have actually needed this initiation, but that he only went through it in order to demonstrate the path to us. Either way, it seems obvious to me that Jesus did go through a number of steps, thereby demonstrating to all of us that the goal of his teaching was to take us through a shift in consciousness. The means for doing this is a gradual path involving a number of initiations.

Let us look at one more example that indicates Jesus might have needed teachers to nudge him along on his path. Read this amazing passage:

> 1 And the third day there was a marriage in Cana of Galilee; and the mother of Jesus was there:
> 2 And both Jesus was called, and his disciples, to the marriage.
> 3 And when they wanted wine, the mother of Jesus saith unto him, They have no wine.
> 4 Jesus saith unto her, Woman, what have I to do with thee? mine hour is not yet come.
> 5 His mother saith unto the servants, Whatsoever he saith unto you, do it. (John, Chapter 2)

When Jesus turned the water into wine at the wedding in Cana, he started his public mission in an irrevocable way. Before that, he seems to have been teaching in secret, but after the wedding, he could no longer hide. It seems Jesus was reluctant to take this decisive step of demonstrating his spiritual powers. He needed his mother to push him over the edge and begin the public part of his mission. To me this makes Jesus much easier to relate to, as it shows he was going through the same hesitation most of us face in life's critical moments.

Why did Jesus take on disciples?

The standard fundamentalist claim is that in order to be saved, we only need to declare Jesus as our Lord and Savior. If that were true, why did Jesus bother taking on disciples?

What was the purpose of Jesus taking disciples? As we have discussed, he obviously gave them a higher teaching than he gave to the multitudes. He also took them through a rather dramatic process that might very well have been a gradual path of initiation where Jesus served as the spiritual master or guru.

Being a direct disciple of Jesus was no picnic. For starters, it required you to break off any kind of normal life and follow Jesus on a wild journey, having no idea where it would take you. It is clear to me that this was not a convenient form of spirituality but a radical path, a crash course. It could easily be seen as a systematic process whereby Jesus sought to break down the egos of his disciples. Just read the scriptures and see how many times Jesus challenged his disciples.

I once had a discussion with a minister in the Danish state church about this very point. The minister was convinced that when Jesus called his disciples, they "had at least a year to get their affairs in order before they actually followed Jesus." Yet Jesus' total mission lasted three years, and he most likely knew he had only a short time to take his disciples to a higher state of consciousness. There simply wasn't time for them to take a year for preparations, and I believe Jesus called his disciples in a rather decisive manner: It's now or never!

Imagine being a fisherman, standing on a hot day on the banks of the Sea of Galilee, mending your nets. Suddenly, a man you have never seen before, a man with long hair and beard and intense eyes, walks up to you and says: "Follow me, and I will make you fishers of men." Then he simply walks away without looking back. Do you scratch your head and wonder what all this is about, or do you recognize this as the calling of a lifetime and instantly follow him—leaving the dead to bury their dead?

Are people ready for Jesus' inner teaching today?

Why did Jesus take on disciples? Compare this to the idea that Jesus taught at two different levels, namely a general teaching for the multitudes and a more advanced teaching for those who were ready for it. I think Jesus recognized that back then most people were not ready for his inner teaching. That is why he publicly gave only a general teaching in the form of parables.

By taking on disciples, Jesus left us a record demonstrating that he was a true initiatic teacher in the ancient tradition. It is surely an irony that mainstream Christianity has labeled this tradition as heretical. We can now reason that what Jesus did to his disciples was a demonstration of how all of us might follow the path to a higher state of consciousness. Jesus used his disciples to set an example of the path we can all follow by becoming his direct disciples. This path is not heresy, it is simply an inner path for those who are ready to take full responsibility for their spiritual growth and salvation.

I am not here trying to say that mainstream Christianity is completely wrong in passing on a general teaching based on Jesus' public discourse. There are still people today who need this outer teaching. I am saying that in my vision Jesus also wanted to leave the record that there is a higher path for those who are ready and willing. I do believe that during the formative centuries of the Roman Catholic Church, this path of initiation was deliberately removed from Christianity, and no later church has restored it.

In my view, Jesus foresaw that there would come a time when millions upon millions of people would be ready for the inner path. I think this time is *now*. I envision that in this age, millions of people are ready to discover and follow the true inner path of being direct disciples of Jesus. How might we become direct disciples of Jesus, since he is no longer on earth? Well, through the comforter, of course, as we have already discussed.

Jesus demonstrated the path we can all follow

My conclusion of this chapter is that although mainstream Christianity has done a lot to remove all records of it, we can still read between the lines and discover the gradual, inner path of Christ. Jesus himself left us a record of an inner path of direct initiations, leading us to a state of consciousness that is as different from normal human awareness as the difference between life and death.

How did he leave us this record, given that the things he expounded to his disciples were never written down? He has done so by demonstrating the path. Jesus taught the path by example. Jesus' entire life can be seen as a public demonstration of the stages we can all follow, the stages that will gradually help us let the human sense of identity die so we are reborn into a distinctly higher sense of identify. Jesus' life and mission symbolize the path that he came to teach us. Even if it is not explained directly in words, we can discover it by reading between the lines.

My conclusion is that Jesus never wanted to be put up on a pedestal where he seemed unreachable to people. He clearly wanted those who were ready for it to see him as an example to follow rather than as an exception that no one can emulate. I see Jesus as an archetype who demonstrated a path that we can all follow.

Think back to the expression "son of man." Jesus did not use this to refer to any and all human beings. Instead, he used it to refer to a person who has awakened to the fact that we all have a higher potential. Jesus referred to himself as the son of man in order to indicate that he himself was never a "normal" human being; he was a person who had started to awaken. He also demonstrated a path whereby he not only saw his higher potential but actually manifested that higher potential. It was by following this process that Jesus qualified himself to be given the title: "Son of God." Jesus came to show us that we all have the potential to move through three stages:

- Man/woman, meaning a person who has not awakened to his or her higher potential. Such a person is still blinded by the consciousness of death and does not have ears to hear the inner teaching of Christ. For people at this stage, Jesus gave his parables and a general teaching that could help them start to see their true potential.

- Son/daughter of Man, meaning a person who has acknowledged that he or she has a higher potential, namely the potential to reach a distinctly higher state of consciousness than the death consciousness. A person at this stage is indeed open to the inner teachings of Christ, even to becoming a direct disciple of Christ through the agency of the comforter.

- Son/daughter of God, meaning a person who has walked the path of Christ, the Way of Life, and has completed the initiations. Such a person has gone through a shift in consciousness and is manifesting his or her highest potential.

I know this is completely beyond the standard Christian model of salvation, but doesn't it explain the following baffling passage from the Gospel of John:

> But as many as received him, to them gave he power to become the sons of God, even to them that believe on his name: (John: 1.12)

With this in mind, let us consider what was the true goal of Jesus' teaching and the path he demonstrated. What state of consciousness did he actually want us to reach?

We might all have been created with
the potential to have the kind of
dominion of mind over matter that Jesus
demonstrated. The difference being that
Jesus had realized
the potential we all have.

10 | DOES JESUS WANT US TO ATTAIN CHRIST CONSCIOUSNESS?

How could we do the works that Jesus did?

As I have said, we have been conditioned to look at Jesus and his teachings through the standard Christian filter. This filter is at its very core affected by the Nicene Creed and the clear tendency to turn Jesus into an exception rather than an example. One might suspect that the standard view of Jesus was created deliberately in order to make it impossible for people to follow his example, but I will let that thought rest until some other time.

Because the standard view portrays Jesus as being completely different from the rest of us, there are some of Jesus' own words that we find it very difficult to explain. Let me give you a primary example of this, namely a passage that I have yet to hear a Christian minister who could interpret in a meaningful way. The reason being that if you accept the standard idolatrous view of Jesus, you simply cannot make sense of what Jesus said here:

> Verily, verily, I say unto you, He that believeth on me, the works that I do shall he do also; and greater works than these shall he do; because I go unto my Father.
> (John: 14.12)

Let us look at the context in which this remark was given. It was a situation where Jesus is talking to his disciples and telling them of certain things that will come to pass, which necessitates him leaving them. Jesus is both comforting them and instructing them in what to do after he has ascended. If you think a little deeper, you see that there are some incredible perspectives hidden in this one paragraph.

First of all, this remark was made to his disciples, meaning people who were following the initiatic path of Christ, the path to a higher state of consciousness. Since I don't speak Greek, I don't know if the words "He that believeth on me" is the best possible translation of the original Greek. I don't know if what was written down is a good translation of what Jesus said in Aramaic. Yet based on what we have discussed, we can propose that the inner meaning is as follows: "Those of you who follow the path I have given you, can attain the state of consciousness I have demonstrated. When you are in the same state of consciousness that I am in, you will be able to do the same works that you have seen me do."

To me that explanation makes sense whereas the standard model can make no sense of this remark. According to the standard model, Jesus was able to perform miracles because he was God from the very beginning and was of the same substance as the father. We were not God from the beginning but were created as sinners. If Jesus had agreed with this view, it would make absolutely no sense for him to tell us that we can do the same works that he did. How can sinners perform the same works as the *only* son of God?

We can all observe that we can't walk on water or turn it into wine, and the reason must be that God created us different from Jesus, right? According to Jesus' inner teaching, the reality might be that we were not created fundamentally different from Jesus. The standard model that elevates Jesus to being so different from us contradicts Genesis:

> And God said, Let us make man in our image, after our likeness: and let them have dominion over ... the earth.
> (Genesis 1:26)

We might all have been created with the potential to have the kind of dominion of mind over matter that Jesus demonstrated. The difference being that Jesus had realized the potential we all have, and that is why he was able to perform the works that he did. Yet if we follow the path taught and demonstrated by Jesus, we will also be able to realize our full potential and do what Jesus did. Not only that, for according to Jesus' own words, we can do even greater works than he did. How do we explain *that*?

Jesus as part of an ancient teaching tradition

As we have seen, there were indeed mystery religions at Jesus' time, and they taught a gradual path to unfolding the full human potential. One of the central elements in these religions – as well as in the ancient guru-chela tradition of India – was that humankind is engaged in a process of gradually raising the collective consciousness. This process is driven by individuals raising their consciousness and pulling everyone else up whereby the whole is gradually raised.

In today's scientific age, it has been proven that all human beings are linked by a collective consciousness. Quantum physics has proven that at the deepest level of matter, there is a form of consciousness with which our minds can interact. It has also proven that at this level, there is no such thing as separate entities—all life is part of an interconnected whole (the principle of non-locality). Obviously, Jesus could not have given a scientific explanation of this 2,000 years ago, but he did give us a pretty obvious hint:

> And I, if I be lifted up from the earth, will draw all men unto me. (John 12:32)

If Jesus really was fundamentally different from us, how would he actually draw us unto him? In today's world we know from science that everything is energy, meaning vibration. If Jesus is to pull us up, he must do so by creating a form of energy that can pull on our minds, even on the collective mind. The only way this can happen is if there is a resonance of vibration between Jesus and us.

If Jesus was fundamentally different from us, science has found no mechanism whereby he could attract us. Yet if Jesus' consciousness is the same as our own, only more developed, then it is indeed possible that by Jesus raising his consciousness, he would create a magnetic pull on the collective consciousness. The more you resonate with Jesus' vibration, the more you will be pulled up by him.

We can now see that Jesus apparently saw himself as part of an ancient tradition of spiritual teachers who served as a kind of forerunners or trailblazers that others could follow. This was the purpose of recognizing John the Baptist as his teacher, thereby showing that Jesus was part of this chain of teachers, which also included some of the Old Testament prophets.

Jesus demonstrated a systematic path whereby we can all raise our consciousness and unlock the full potential with which we were created. He did this so that we could see what was possible for us also. Beyond that, Jesus also seems to have recognized that by him following the path, his victory over the death consciousness would serve to raise the collective consciousness. This would make it possible for others to build on Jesus' accomplishments and thereby do "greater works" than Jesus had demonstrated. As the collective consciousness is raised, things become possible that simply were not possible in the past.

In my view, this makes it much easier for me to relate to Jesus, and how could a path to a higher state of consciousness ever become obsolete? It is precisely such a path that millions of spiritual people are seeking in today's world. The only problem being that so far few have been able to find it in Jesus' teachings. To me, that is a very sad degradation of Jesus.

One last point. The above quote also demonstrates that Jesus had no desire to set himself up on a pedestal for all eternity. He was a true teacher, and what is the goal of a true teacher? It is to raise the students to the same level of consciousness as that reached by the teacher. When they build on that foundation, they can reach even higher than the teacher. The goal of a true teacher is to take the students to a point where they no longer need the teacher. A true teacher seeks to make the students independent and self-sufficient.

Given that Jesus also gave us the comforter, I don't see how a Jesus that teaches us a path to a higher state of consciousness could ever become obsolete. That is, if we are willing to follow the real Jesus instead of the idol created by mainstream Christianity.

What was Jesus' level of consciousness?

Let us take one more look at Jesus' statement that we have the potential to do the works that he did. I admit that I haven't actually tried to walk on water, and the reason is that I don't really believe I could do it. Yet why don't I think I can do what Jesus did? Let us turn the question around: "If Jesus was right that we have the potential to do the works that he did, then we obviously are not there yet. What would it take for us to get to the point where we could unlock this potential?"

To me, the answer is obvious: We would have to go through a fundamental shift in consciousness so that we were in the same state of consciousness as Jesus. This is, of course, another thought that the standard model will label as blasphemous and heretical. But would Jesus agree?

We really have only two options. According to the scriptures – which mainstream Christians consider authoritative, perhaps even the infallible word of God – Jesus did say that if we fulfill certain requirements, we can do the works that he did. This leaves us with two options: Either Jesus was lying or he was telling the truth.

If Jesus was telling the truth, it follows that we do actually have the potential to attain the mastery of "mind over matter" that Jesus demonstrated. However, it is obvious that we cannot do those works right now, and the reason is that we are still trapped in the consciousness of death. If we allow Jesus to take us on a systematic path, we can awaken from that state of consciousness and be reborn into a higher state of consciousness. In this new state of consciousness, we can indeed do the kind of works that Jesus demonstrated.

Jesus did not come to show us a state of consciousness that only he could have (because he was so different from us). He came to demonstrate a state of consciousness that it is natural for us to have because God created us with the same creative potential. God did this because it is his good pleasure to give us the kingdom.

To me it always seemed odd that a good God would send Jesus to earth and essentially say: "Here is my one and only son. I am sending him down to you so that you can all see how perfect he is compared to you, and thereby really feel like the miserable sinners you are—the miserable sinners that I – in my infinite goodness – created you to be." This never made sense to me, but if God sent Jesus to show me a potential that I can develop by following the path demonstrated by Jesus, now that *does* indeed make sense to me.

What do we call the state of consciousness that Jesus wants us to attain? Doesn't it seem natural to call it the "Christ consciousness?" Jesus wants all of us to attain the same state of consciousness as himself. He wants all of us to be the Christ on earth, the Christ in embodiment.

Has Jesus failed as a teacher?

Again, we hear the roar of "blasphemy," "heresy" and "works of the devil," but are we going to let that intimidate us into denying our potential to follow the path outlined by Jesus himself? Not as far as I am concerned. For 1600 years, mainstream Christianity has succeeded in intimidating people into denying their Christ potential and that is long enough. It is time and high time for those of us who are willing to take a stand and give Jesus the victory he deserves, the victory of seeing millions of people discover, accept and follow his inner teachings.

To me, it is completely obvious that Jesus was a true teacher, and what is the ultimate victory of a true teacher? It is to duplicate himself by raising his students to the same level of mastery that he had reached. What Jesus was really saying was: "When you follow the path I have given you and reach the level of consciousness I demonstrated, then you will do the works that I did and even greater works than I did. And that is when I will know I have been successful as a teacher!"

Truly, if no one dares to follow in his footsteps, Jesus will have failed as a teacher. I personally don't want Jesus to fail. If I can contribute to his victory by raising my own state of consciousness, then I am willing to do so, no matter what mainstream Christian preachers might say about it. My response to mainstream Christianity is simple: "You don't own me, and you were never granted a patent on Jesus!" The reason being that both Jesus and the Christ consciousness are beyond what any power structure on earth can control. The Christ consciousness is beyond anything on this little planet, and it is high time we acknowledged this cosmic fact.

How did Jesus see himself

Once again, I want to use our modern knowledge of the human ego. The ego is on a never-ending quest for security, and as a result, it wants to elevate one religion to being the superior religion on earth. Since Christianity is obviously focused on Jesus, the ego wants to elevate Jesus to a superior status, meaning he must be the only one who has ever attained the Christ consciousness. To the ego, Jesus simply *must* be special, for otherwise how can the ego feel that Jesus can do something for it that it cannot do for itself?

When I look at Jesus, I see a person who has transcended the ego-based consciousness. To me, that does make him very special, although not in the sense that no one else could ever rise above the ego. I see that we all have the potential to rise above ego, and I see that this is part of what Jesus wanted to teach us. Precisely because Jesus himself had risen above ego,

10 | Does Jesus Want Us to Attain Christ Consciousness? 145

I think he had a very realistic assessment of who and what he was and wasn't.

I have already mentioned the situation where a person calls him "good master" and Jesus makes it clear that only God deserves to be called good. Now take a look at these quotes:

> I can of mine own self do nothing: (John 5:30)

> The Son can do nothing of himself, (John 5:19)

> My Father worketh hitherto, and I work. (John 5:17)

> ... but the Father that dwelleth in me, he doeth the works. (John 14:10)

When I read these and other statements made by Jesus, it is clear to me that Jesus never allowed himself to believe that he personally had the power to do the works that were done. He clearly saw this as a higher power working through him, a power that he did not own or control. It is clear that Jesus had no desire to control this power, nor did he think it was possible. Only the ego wants to control the power of God, and only people blinded by the ego think they can do so.

I see Jesus as a person with a very realistic self-assessment. Jesus knew he was a human being and that he was never created with any special status. He had no ego-based need to have or claim such a status. Jesus also knew that he had risen above the normal human state of consciousness, namely the death consciousness in which one is blinded by the illusions of the ego. As a result, Jesus had become an open door whereby a higher power could work through him. This power could do works that people in a normal state of consciousness cannot perform. That is why Jesus made it clear that his own power was as nothing. He also realized that because he had done the work of raising his consciousness, his father could work through him.

Jesus seems to have made a clear distinction between himself as an embodied being and the power or Spirit of God. He never claimed the two were "of the same substance," nor did he think he could control the power of God.

Did Jesus always talk about himself?

I know that any fundamentalist Christian would immediately refer to the following verse:

> Jesus saith unto him, I am the way, the truth, and the life: no man cometh unto the Father, but by me. (John 14:6)

This is the one verse that more than anything else has been used to justify the belief that Christianity is the only true religion and the only road to salvation. This belief has probably caused more warfare and violence than any other single belief in world history. The real question to ask here is whether this statement can be understood at a deeper level.

Compare this to what I just said about Jesus making a clear distinction between himself and something beyond himself, something that is beyond any human being yet is capable of expressing itself through a human being who has risen to a certain level of consciousness. Is it possible that it is not Jesus as a physical, historical person who is the "way, the truth and the life" but that it is the Spirit that is the way, the truth and the life? Were these words actually spoken by the Spirit through the human vehicle of Jesus?

Were they meant to indicate that if the rest of us want to find the way that leads to the truth and to eternal life, we

10 | Does Jesus Want Us to Attain Christ Consciousness?

have to do what Jesus did, namely put on the same state of consciousness that Jesus had attained? Now take another statement that is rather baffling if you take it literally:

> Jesus said unto them, Verily, verily, I say unto you, Before Abraham was, I am. (John 8:58)

If you insist that the Bible should be "interpreted literally," you literally cannot make sense of this. We know from other Bible verses that Jesus was born at a specific historical time, and Catholic doctrine specifically denies the idea of the pre-existence of souls. So how could Jesus possibly be older than Abraham? If this was the Spirit speaking through Jesus, then there is obviously no problem. With this in mind, let us look at a rather mystical and mystifying passage from John:

> 1 In the beginning was the Word, and the Word was with God, and the Word was God.
> 2 The same was in the beginning with God.
> 3 All things were made by him; and without him was not any thing made that was made.
> 4 In him was life; and the life was the light of men.
> 5 And the light shineth in darkness; and the darkness comprehended it not. (John, Chapter 1)

Because of what comes later, the standard Christian model says that this must somehow refer to Jesus, but I don't see that as the only possibility. First of all, as many scholars have pointed out, a better translation of the original Greek would be "Logos" instead of "Word." The Logos is by the ancient mystery religions seen as the overall principle that governs the unfoldment of the entire universe. The Logos is clearly beyond any single human being.

I think Jesus was aware of the difference between the Spirit or Logos and himself as a being who was incarnate on earth. He did not for one minute allow himself to believe that the totality of the Logos had incarnated in and as himself. He recognized that by attaining a higher state of consciousness, he had become the open door whereby the Logos could express itself on earth. He did not allow himself the spiritual arrogance of thinking he was the same as the Logos. If we look at this in a slightly different way, I think it becomes easier to wrap our minds around it.

Let us stop being so focused on ourselves

One of the great advantages we have today compared to people of Jesus' time is that we know a lot more about the universe in which we live. We know that we are living on a planet that is like a speck of dust in an infinite universe. Therefore, we should be able to overcome the mindset that was so dominant in previous ages, namely the tendency to think that we live in the center of the universe and thus we must be oh-so important to God.

If you read the Old Testament with a bit of honesty, you can clearly see that the ancient Jews believed the ultimate God was intimately concerned about their everyday affairs and would even support their massacres of neighboring tribes. During the Middle Ages, most Christians believed the earth was a flat disc with a dome above it, and the sun, moon and stars were painted on the inside of the dome. If you physically traveled up from the earth, you would break through the dome to heaven where the ultimate God would be waiting to welcome you with great fanfare.

We now know a very different reality where we are not nearly as central in God's creation. Based on this, we should be able to see that the idea that the ultimate God, the very Logos that guided the creation of the entire universe, came down to earth in its entirety and incarnated here in one specific man 2,000 years ago is, well, how shall we put it ... a bit unrealistic? I think we should even be able to see that Jesus himself would be appalled by the idea that he was the incarnation of "the God of very God." Can we find a more realistic explanation?

I see the Word, Logos or Spirit as a specific form of consciousness, namely what I like to call the Universal Christ consciousness. I also see that the Gospel of John gives us an important clue for understanding the function of the Universal Christ consciousness. It was literally the guiding principle that God used for designing the entire universe. Therefore, "All things were made by the Christ consciousness; and without the Christ consciousness was not any thing made that was made." The Universal Christ consciousness is embedded within every "thing," meaning it is actually here with us right now. We can never be separated from it in reality; only in our minds.

We might say that the Christ consciousness has two aspects, a universal aspect that is beyond any human being and a personal aspect that is available to any human being. For most of us, the Christ consciousness is only a potential because it has not yet been expressed. How do we personally express the Christ consciousness? We do so by following the way taught and demonstrated by Jesus.

Jesus never intended to set himself up as the only human being who ever had become and ever could become an open door for the Christ consciousness. The entire purpose for Jesus' mission was to show us the potential we all have. When we follow the path outlined by Jesus, the Christ will be born in our hearts. We then become the Christ incarnate, we become the individual or personal aspect of Christ. The "body" of the Universal Christ consciousness will be broken in and as us.

Jesus was an archetypal example of a person who has become an open door for the Universal Christ consciousness to express itself on earth. That is precisely why the Universal Christ consciousness made certain statements through Jesus that were meant to tell us something about itself. The physical Jesus did not exist before Abraham, nor was Jesus the way, the truth and the life, nor was Jesus the light which lights every man that comes into the world, nor was Jesus the only way to the father.

In reality, all such statements were made by the Universal Christ consciousness through Jesus, and their inner meaning is that if we want to get to the kingdom of God, we have to enter through the only door there is, namely the individualized Christ consciousness. Where do we find that door? Do we find it in a man who lived 2,000 years ago and is no longer physically here? Or do we find it where Jesus himself told us to look for it: within us?

Jesus was not the totality of the Universal Christ consciousness; he was an open door for it. Jesus came to show us that each of us have the potential to become the open door for the universal Christ consciousness. Only by personally becoming the open door for the universal Christ consciousness will we be able to enter the kingdom. The only way you are going to be saved is that you put on the Christ consciousness so that you too become the Christ incarnate.

The ego rears its ugly head

I am, of course, aware that the idea that Jesus was the exclusive incarnation is one of mainstream Christianity's most sacred holy cows, but I think it is time to put the poor animal out to pasture. I think Jesus himself would have reacted as strongly to this idea as he did when the Jews sought to kill him for speaking blasphemy:

> Ye are of your father the devil, and the lusts of your father ye will do. He was a murderer from the beginning, and abode not in the truth, because there is no truth in him. When he speaketh a lie, he speaketh of his own: for he is a liar, and the father of it. (John 8:44)

I believe the primary lie of the "father of lies" is that the Universal Christ consciousness is *not* here on earth, meaning that the earth is separated from God and thus belongs to the "prince of this world." In order to keep control over the earth, the devil must keep all people trapped in the death consciousness in which we deny our Christ potential. When Jesus publicly declared that he was the Christ, the devil had two plans. Plan A was to kill Jesus physically in order to shut him up. Plan B was to kill Jesus as an example so that no one else would follow in his footsteps.

The devil must at all cost prevent any human being from becoming the Christ incarnate. The devil would much have preferred that Jesus had never attained the Christ consciousness or had never declared this openly. Since he could not prevent Jesus from becoming the Christ, he wants to make sure that no one else will ever do so. The way to accomplish this is to actually use Jesus' personal victory to prevent the personal victory of anyone else. This can be accomplished by claiming that Jesus was the *exclusive* incarnation and that saying you can follow his example is blasphemy.

As long as people believe this, the devil has won and Jesus' victory is put on hold. Yet will it be put on hold forever? Not if I can help it. How about you?

Was no one saved before Jesus?

Let me revisit the statement: "I am the way, the truth and the life, no one cometh to the father save by me." I know this is the one sentence that many Christians will use as a justification for refuting that anyone else can attain the Christ consciousness.

Let us take this statement and interpret it literally. If we do, we must reason that before Jesus came to earth – and supposedly bought our release from sin through the spilling of his blood on the cross – salvation simply was not an option. This must mean that before Jesus incarnated as a physical, historical person, no soul had ever been saved.

This is a rather strange thought because it would mean that a supposedly good God created the earth and sent many souls here. Those souls were condemned to *not* be saved because God's only son had not yet been born on earth. Aside from this common-sense perspective, this idea also contradicts the Bible. Here is one obvious example:

> 17 And after six days Jesus taketh Peter, James, and John his brother, and bringeth them up into an high mountain apart,
> 2 And was transfigured before them: and his face did shine as the sun, and his raiment was white as the light.
> 3 And, behold, there appeared unto them Moses and Elias talking with him. (Matthew, Chapter 17)

How do you explain that Moses and Elias appeared to Jesus, unless Moses and Elias had been saved and now lived in heaven, from where they could appear to Jesus? If no soul could be saved before Jesus had been crucified, then how could the souls of Moses and Elias appear as obviously spiritual beings?

10 | Does Jesus Want Us to Attain Christ Consciousness?

What if the key to salvation is the Universal Christ consciousness? Since this was there from the beginning of creation, and thus existed even before Abraham, it is logical that salvation has been an option since the first souls incarnated on earth. What Jesus did was not to make salvation possible; what he did was to make it much more obvious how to attain salvation.

My understanding is that before Jesus came, attaining the Christ consciousness was much more difficult and only very few people reached the goal. Because Jesus did manifest the Christ consciousness, he created a shift that made the Christ consciousness a realistic potential for many more people.

Unfortunately, the very religion that claims to be the only true representative of Jesus has completely obscured this fact. But then again, since the Christ consciousness is everywhere present, what can prevent us from rediscovering the true purpose of Jesus' coming? The Christ consciousness is the open door, which no man – and no church – can shut. Well, in a sense all of us can shut the door by denying the Universal Christ consciousness the opportunity to express itself through us. Of course, doing this is the real blasphemy because we are all killing Christ within ourselves.

People who are not ready to accept full responsibility for their salvation need a religion that will validate this inability or unwillingness to accept responsibility.

11 WHY ARE WE IN THE DEATH CONSCIOUSNESS?

Why do we – really – need to be saved?

I earlier brought up the question of why we need to be saved, and we can now take a second look. Let me be a bit personal. I have had inner, mystical experiences that to me confirm beyond any doubt that God exists. Those experiences also confirmed to me that God is completely and utterly beyond the Old Testament angry God in the sky. The real God is a God of love—unconditional love. The real God simply cannot be put into any mental box created by us human beings here on earth.

As a result of these experiences, one thing is clear to me. The real God did *not* create me as a sinner. The entire idea of original sin, meaning that I was born into sin because of what Adam and Eve did, is a complete fabrication. It has absolutely no divine authority or reality because it was another political idea defined by the Roman Catholic Church in order to control people.

Having said that, I don't believe I am ready to walk into the kingdom of heaven at this moment. I recognize that I have not yet attained the state of consciousness that Jesus demonstrated—the state of consciousness that is the *only* key to entering heaven. The question now becomes: How did I end up being in a lower state of consciousness? Or to be more specific: Did God create me in a lower state of consciousness, or did I enter it in some other way?

For many years, I have worked hard to develop my ability to attune to the comforter and get answers from within myself. As a result of this process, it has become clear to me that God did not create me as a sinner and the devil did not force me into sin. Instead, God created me as a self-aware being with free will. I then used my free will to descend into a lower state of consciousness. I was not created in the death consciousness nor was I forced or fooled into falling into it. I descended into the death consciousness as a result of my own choices. God is not responsible for my situation—*I am!*

Taking responsibility for yourself

Based on my 36 years of interacting with religious and spiritual people, it is clear to me that this will be the most provocative remark I have made so far in this book. When you step back and look at religious and spiritual people, you can see a clear dividing line between those who are ready to take full responsibility for their salvation and those who are not ready—but still need to place that responsibility somewhere outside themselves.

Once again, I am not seeking to blame anyone. It has been my experience that accepting full and final responsibility for our own salvation is probably the hardest thing we can do as human beings. The reason is very simple. The one underlying characteristic of the death consciousness is that it makes it seem real to us that we don't have full responsibility for our salvation. The essence of the death consciousness is that it places

11 Why Are We in the Death Consciousness?

the responsibility for our salvation outside ourselves. The essence of the consciousness of Life, the Christ consciousness, is that it places all responsibility inside ourselves—where Jesus said the doorway to the kingdom of God is located.

In today's age, it is my observation that millions upon millions of people are ready to accept full responsibility for their salvation and many have already done so. We now see a fundamental divide between two types of spiritual needs:

• People who are not ready to accept full responsibility for their salvation need a religion that will validate this inability or unwillingness to accept responsibility. They need a religion that tells them that they did not cause themselves to go into a lower state of consciousness, and they cannot get themselves out of it. They were either created that way, or they were forced or fooled by the devil. They need an external savior in order to get out of their present state of consciousness and enter heaven. Such people need exactly the kind of pacifying religion that Christianity has been since the formation of the Roman Catholic Church.

• People who are ready to accept responsibility can no longer be satisfied by a pacifying religion. They need a philosophy that can show them a viable, systematic path for raising their consciousness to the point where they are ready to enter a higher realm. They simply will not believe in the promises of an external salvation because they know from inner experience that the promises are not real.

It is my clear observation that in today's age, millions of people are ready for a self-empowering form of spirituality. I see that many of the people who grew up in a Christian culture, but have left mainstream Christianity behind, are among them. I also see that there are still many of these people who are trying to hang on to their Christian faith, and they struggle to find a deeper meaning behind what they know are empty doctrines and rituals.

I think it is high time for the appearance of a new form of Christianity that is designed to use Jesus' inner teachings as a way to fulfill the spiritual needs of these people. As I have argued, the purpose of Jesus' inner teachings was to offer people a systematic, initiatic path to a higher state of consciousness. There really can be only one explanation for the fact that this inner path was stamped out by mainstream churches: Christianity has been dominated by people who are blinded by the death consciousness.

Let us take a look at how this can happen. How do we explain that we can all be blinded by the death consciousness to the point where we don't even realize how blind we are?

Does life have a (believable) purpose?

It is my vision that when future historians look back at our time, one of the things they will be astonished by is that they see a society with a very high level of technological sophistication, yet that same society failed to bring up its children with the sense that life has a believable purpose. Take a look at a fact mentioned earlier, namely that mental health problems are on the rise in most developed nations. Many of these problems can be directly traced to the fact that young people have not been brought up to feel that life has a purpose and that what they do matters. How did we get to that point?

You don't have to know a lot about history to see that it is caused by a combination of medieval Christian doctrines

11 Why Are We in the Death Consciousness?

and materialistic ideas. Mainstream Christianity stamped out the inner teachings of Jesus, which outlined life as a systematic path towards a higher state of consciousness. Such a path really is the only way to provide people with a sense of purpose in life, as proven by the millions of spiritual people who have precisely found a sense of meaning by following such a path. When you realize that you have the potential to rise to a state of consciousness in which you are beyond all human misery, your life does take on a new meaning. Suddenly, everything you do matters because you can learn from any situation and use it as a stepping stone for raising your consciousness.

What early Christians did was to remove this inner path from Christianity, and that meant official Christianity simply could not provide a very sophisticated explanation for the purpose of life. Instead, we are left with some half-baked explanations about us living for the glorification of God—that same angry God in the sky who created us as sinners and will send some of us to hell. I don't think this explanation was ever believable to people, but it is certainly less believable today than it ever was.

After Christianity had removed the inner path, it had taken away the sense that life has a long-term spiritual purpose. When scientific materialism entered the stage, people already had a low sense of purpose. Many people now became susceptible to accepting the materialistic idea that we are simply evolved monkeys, living in a universe where everything – including our existence – is the result of random events. In a random universe, life cannot have any meaning at all. Why shouldn't young people who have grown up in such a culture seek to dull their sense of meaninglessness with drugs or alcohol? I mean, what is there to live for?

As I have said, I truly love the real Jesus and I know he has answers to all of life's questions. It is obvious to me that

Jesus also has a believable answer to the question: "What is the purpose of life?"

The way I currently see that answer is that we are self-aware beings. We were created at a certain level of self-awareness, but we were also created with the potential to raise our consciousness to a distinctly higher level. Our self-awareness may seem like a burden, but that is only because it is currently focused on the death consciousness. By following Christ as our inner teacher, we can gradually raise ourselves above the death consciousness, and we can then attain the consciousness of life, the Christ consciousness.

In this state, we will feel at one with our spiritual source and at one with all life. Not only is this a wonderful state of consciousness to be in, it also gives us a supreme sense of purpose. For people who have started to awaken from the death consciousness, the process of raising their consciousness will give them a profound and believable sense of purpose and meaning.

After reflecting on this for many years, I see no way to give people a sense of meaning unless you also give them the perspective of a systematic path for raising their consciousness beyond their current level. Unless Christianity can give modern people a believable sense of purpose, how can it meet their spiritual needs? It just can't be done!

Contradictions or symbolism?

One of the characteristics of the death consciousness is precisely that when you are truly blinded by it, you can see no purpose or meaning to life. How did we ever get so far into the death consciousness that we think life is meaningless? In order to understand that, I think we should go back and take a look at what really happened in the Garden of Eden.

11 | Why Are We in the Death Consciousness?

One of the themes in this book is that because official Christianity removed Jesus' inner teachings, there are many questions that it cannot answer. This is disastrous in today's age because we have been conditioned by the cause-and-effect mindset to look for explanations that make sense. Because we have also adopted the linear, analytical way of thinking, we look for contradictions. And there are lots of contradictions in the world-view presented by official Christianity, what I have called the standard model.

We all know the story of how Adam and Eve were cast out of paradise and had two sons, Cain and Abel. Cain then killed Abel and here is what happened next:

> 16 And Cain went out from the presence of the Lord, and dwelt in the land of Nod, on the east of Eden.
> 17 And Cain knew his wife; and she conceived, and bare Enoch: and he builded a city, and called the name of the city, after the name of his son, Enoch. (Genesis, Chapter 4)

If you read this story with a linear mindset, a logical question must come up: "Where did Cain's wife come from?" The Bible – which some say should be interpreted literally – tells us there were only two people in Eden, namely Adam and Eve. They had two sons, which means that according to a literal interpretation, the total population of the earth at that time would have been four people. After Cain kills Abel, the population is reduced to three. Then suddenly, Cain finds a wife, and from them all the rest of us have descended.

My purpose here is not in any way to say this proves the Bible is contradictory and thus worthless in its entirety. My purpose is to say that the Bible was never meant to be read with a literal, linear mindset. The Bible is a spiritual text, and it is meant to be seen as a symbolic representation that can be understood at several levels, ranging from a superficial level towards deeper and deeper levels of understanding.

Let us take a look at what we might learn by going towards a deeper, symbolic interpretation of Genesis. Some might say that in the following I will reinvent the creation story, but then again, is that necessarily wrong?

Was the Garden of Eden a mystery school?

I have already mentioned the quote from Genesis where God says we are created in his image and after his likeness and that we are created to have dominion over the earth. We can interpret this to mean that we are created with a set of creative abilities, yet we were not created with these abilities fully developed. We were created with the potential to expand our self-awareness until we would have the kind of dominion of mind over matter that Jesus demonstrated.

One consequence of this view is that planet earth, and indeed the entire material universe, now becomes a giant laboratory that is designed to help us develop our creative abilities. What does that say about the Garden of Eden? What if the Garden was not the fully developed, perfect, never-changing paradise that most Christians think it was? What if the Garden of Eden was a kind of educational institution in which the figure that Genesis calls "God" was actually a spiritual teacher?

We were created with a limited self-awareness, which gave us limited creative abilities. God did not simply throw us into the earth to either sink or swim. Instead, we were placed in a protected environment in which we were under the direct supervision of a spiritual teacher. This teacher offered us a systematic path whereby we would gradually increase our creative abilities by passing a series of initiations. In the Genesis story,

11 Why Are We in the Death Consciousness?

these initiations are symbolized by the different trees or fruits in the garden.

This brings up an entirely new explanation for a question that is surely one of the most baffling aspects of the Garden of Eden story: "Why did a supposedly good God allow the Tree of Knowledge to be in the garden?" We probably all remember the story where God had told Adam and Eve that they could eat of all of the fruits except one because if they ate of that tree, they would "surely die." If God didn't want them to eat of the tree, why plant it in the garden in the first place; why not simply leave it out?

The explanation that now emerges is that the Tree of Knowledge is a symbol for a particular initiation. Given that the tree was in the garden, it was an initiation that Adam and Eve would eventually take. Yet because of the nature of this initiation, they were not meant to take it until they were ready for it. If they took the initiation before being ready, they would surely fail it and thus have to leave the school.

I know this raises other questions, and I will address them shortly. For now, let me give you this thought. Imagine that the Garden of Eden was a mystery school in which souls were meant to go through a series of progressively more advanced initiations. The final initiation was to deal with the "knowledge of good and evil." Some souls took this initiation before they were ready for it, and as a result they failed the initiation. The consequence was that – not as the punishment of an angry God but as a result of their own choices – they descended into the death consciousness in which they could no longer perceive the mystery school.

Ever since then, these souls have had to grow outside the protected environment of the mystery school. Instead of having the direct guidance of a loving teacher, they have been left to learn by seeing how the material universe responds to their state of consciousness, which we might call the School of Hard Knocks. Because we have been blinded by the death consciousness, the knocks have indeed been very hard. To make matters worse, we have been so blind that we have had no idea what is really going on.

What Jesus came to do was to re-establish the initiatic path from the original mystery school. He came to offer us this path in our present level of blindness, and this was and is indeed a major grace offered to us. Yet because people were so blinded by the death consciousness, they were not ready to accept this path in its fullness. The reason being that they were not ready to accept full responsibility for their own salvation, for their own state of consciousness. They failed to understand what was truly offered by Jesus, and this even caused official Christianity to lose the inner path of Christ.

What if we have now reached a point in our collective growth where more and more people are ready to accept the inner path of Christ? What if more people are ready to accept responsibility for their own growth? What if more people are ready to re-enter the Garden of Eden and receive direct, inner guidance from a spiritual teacher—a comforter? Surely, this raises some questions, so let us look at one of the crucial ones.

How does the Garden of Eden story relate to us?

I earlier said that in today's world, you can't expect people to accept a Jesus who seems to have no direct relationship to their personal lives. The same, of course, holds true for the Garden of Eden story. What's it gotta do with me?

If we recognize that the story is meant to be understood as a symbol, we can now see that it actually gives us a symbolic representation of what has happened to all of us. We are all beings who started out in a protected environment under the guidance of a spiritual teacher. We all chose to eat the forbidden fruit, which is a symbol for us partaking of the death consciousness and thus losing awareness of our true identity as spiritual beings. That is precisely why we find ourselves here on earth and why we need the inner path of Christ that can help us climb back to an awareness of who we really are and where we came from. It is also why we need the comforter, who will bring "all things to our remembrance" that Jesus wants us to know.

Of course, this raises another question, because surely most of us don't remember ever being in a mystery school and sneaking into the schoolmaster's yard to eat some forbidden fruit. When did this supposedly happen? We will look at that in the next chapter.

❧

Jesus is a unique teacher
of the inner path of initiation.

❧

12 | EXPLAINING THE DEEPER QUESTIONS OF LIFE

When did we all eat the forbidden fruit?

I earlier said that because official Christianity has "lost" the inner path taught by Jesus, there are many things which the standard world-view simply cannot explain. For example, it cannot really explain why we are so different. Why is one person born with tremendous talents while another is born with insurmountable handicaps?

If our souls came into being shortly after the conception of our present physical bodies, how do we explain our differences? The only option for the standard model is to say that God created us that way, but that leaves the question of why a supposedly good God would create people with such different qualities. I mean, why would God want to favor *me* and punish *you?*

Obviously, the inner teachings of Jesus have an explanation, but what might it be? Let me ask you to read the following quote:

> 1 And as Jesus passed by, he saw a man which was blind from his birth.
> 2 And his disciples asked him, saying, Master, who did sin, this man, or his parents that he was born blind?
> 3 Jesus answered, Neither hath this man sinned, nor his parents: but that the works of God should be made manifest in him. (John, Chapter 9)

According to the standard model, it makes absolutely no sense that Jesus' disciples would ask him whether a man could be born blind because of his own sin. When would the soul of this man have sinned? I have heard a Christian minister speculating that the soul must have sinned in the womb. How does it make any sense that a fetus in the womb – who can't see – could commit a sin so severe that God would punish it by having it be born blind? Why would a good God ever do something like that?

Were the disciples just babbling here, or is there a deeper explanation? Consider what we have already seen, namely that Jesus gave a simplified teaching for the public, but that he privately gave a more advanced teaching to his disciples. Is it possible that according to the inner teaching given to the disciples, this question makes perfect sense? If so, what might that inner teaching be?

One possible answer is that the man had sinned before being born because the man's soul had been incarnated before. The man had sinned in a past lifetime, a previous incarnation.

I know all mainstream Christians have been programmed to reject the concept of reincarnation as the works of the devil, and we will shortly look at why the early Roman church was so dead-set against this idea. For now, let us consider that reincarnation might also explain another baffling statement made by Jesus to his disciples:

> 10 And his disciples asked him, saying, Why then say the scribes that Elias must first come?
> 11 And Jesus answered and said unto them, Elias truly shall first come, and restore all things.
> 12 But I say unto you that Elias is come already, and they knew him not, but have done unto him whatsoever they listed. Likewise shall also the Son of man suffer of them.
> 13 Then the disciples understood that he spake unto them of John the Baptist. (Matthew, Chapter 17)

Here Jesus is directly saying – and again this is said to his disciples in private – that John the Baptist was the Old Testament prophet Elias "come again." How do you come again? The Bible doesn't say that John the Baptist was born of a virgin or through divine intercession. He was born in the normal way, so how could John be Elias come again unless John was a reincarnation of the same soul that was Elias in a past life?

As another example of the explanatory power of reincarnation, let me reach back to my opening question of why we are so different. When you accept reincarnation, you see that God did not create one person privileged and another handicapped. God created us all equal, but over many lifetimes we have created our current situations. My situation is not the result of the punishment or favors of a fickle God. It is the result of my own choices made over many lifetimes.

My current situation is the result of a long path, and the purpose of it is my soul's growth. Some people have made destructive choices over many lifetimes, and this has created a downward spiral that explains why they were born with certain limitations in this lifetime. By following the inner path offered by Jesus, they can reverse the spiral and start growing towards a higher state of consciousness. If reincarnation can explain such deep questions, why isn't it part of Christianity? Again, the standard Christian historical filter gives us a distorted view of the history of Christianity. Reincarnation was indeed part of early Christianity, and Jesus might well have taught it to his disciples. Let us take a look at why it is no longer part of Christianity.

Why didn't the early Church like reincarnation?

Let me first give you some indisputable historical facts. At Jesus' own time, one of the major Jewish sects was the Pharisees and they taught reincarnation. I earlier mentioned that Jesus might have been associated with the Essene community. The Essenes taught reincarnation. I also mentioned that Jesus might have traveled to the East, and you don't have to go too far East to encounter Hinduism, Taoism and Buddhism, which all teach reincarnation.

I also mentioned that there were a number of mystery religions at Jesus time, and they generally taught reincarnation. The idea of a path of initiation really only reaches its full potential when combined with reincarnation. The initiations you go through on the mystical path are partly geared towards setting you free from the choices (sins, if you will) from past lives. You can then complete the initiatic path on earth and ascend to a higher realm, having no need to reincarnate.

In the first centuries of the Christian religion, reincarnation was an idea that was accepted by a number of Christian sects and theologians. Some Gnostics were among them, and they have, of course, been labeled as heretics by the Church. Yet quite a few theologians who were mainstream at their own time either believed in or openly discussed reincarnation. Among them were: St. Augustine, Clement of Alexandria, St. Gregory of Nyssa, Justin Martyr, and St. Jerome.

The foremost proponent of reincarnation was a man named Origin of Alexandria. Between the third and the fifth century, Origen was one of the theological giants of Christianity, and his writings were read widely. In the sixth century, Origin was banned as a heretic, mainly because he taught reincarnation. This happened in the year 553, and it was in part instigated by Theodora, the Wife of the Roman emperor Justinian. Once again, we see the influence of Roman emperors on the Roman Catholic Church.

Again, it is not my intent here to provide a long historical discourse because the facts about the banning of reincarnation are well documented and easy to find in books and on the Internet. The question I want to go into is why the Roman Church wanted to ban reincarnation?

I really don't think we can understand this without reaching back to my previous claim that the Roman Church was a political institution, designed to control the masses—exactly as the Jewish religion whose leaders had Jesus killed. As I have hinted before, the most effective way to control the population is through a combination of physical power and belief, such as religious belief. In this case, the Roman emperor obviously had the physical power, although he had trouble controlling the entire Roman population in this way alone. He needed the help of the Church, which provided the ideological basis for control.

This was done by creating a belief system claiming that people were sinners by nature because they were created as such by a supposedly good and just God. This God would punish all sinners by an eternity of torment in a fiery hell. A good God had created people with a fundamental deficit. From birth all people were predisposed to go to hell, unless they had some external intercession.

The only way to avoid hell, and instead be rewarded by a privileged life in heaven, was to be set free from your sins. There was only one way to be free from sins, and it was controlled by the Roman Catholic Church. If you wanted to avoid hell and enter heaven, you had to be obedient to church leaders—and thus also to the emperor.

In order to make this scheme believable to all people, church leaders had to stamp out reincarnation. The reason being that they needed people to believe that salvation is a "one-shot deal." Only if people believed they had this one lifetime to secure their salvation, would they submit fully to the authority of the Church.

The belief in reincarnation undercuts a centralized authority by placing responsibility for salvation with the people themselves. What determines your entry into heaven is not the approval of a church authority here on earth; it is exclusively your state of consciousness. In order to enter heaven, you have to attain a higher state of consciousness (as I have argued, you have to attain the Christ consciousness demonstrated by Jesus). If you do not attain this in one lifetime, you have the opportunity to come back and work on it in one or several future lifetimes. Salvation is not a one-shot deal so there is less incentive to submit to a Church authority, which promises that it can guarantee your salvation after this lifetime.

Can reincarnation explain central mysteries?

The standard model has created certain questions that simply cannot be answered within the framework of the model itself. A prime example is the existence of evil and why some people are born privileged and other disadvantaged.

According to the standard view, God is good and just. Why would a just God allow evil to exist and to create such monstrous conditions on this planet? Why doesn't God wipe out evil, and why did he allow it in the first place? Why would a supposedly just God allow children to be born with severe physical diseases or handicaps, or be born into such horrendous conditions that it virtually guarantees a life of suffering?

These are questions that Christians – theologians and "ordinary" people alike – have been speculating about for centuries. If you keep your considerations within the mental box defined by official Christianity, you simply cannot find a meaningful answer. As a result, many people – and I think a growing number of people – have become so disillusioned that they have decided to leave all religion behind and become atheists or agnostics. Once again, I see that Jesus' inner teachings have answers that can explain this.

We can now see that evil is not created by God. Because we were created as souls who have free will, evil is a possibility. Evil is created as a result of choice. When you choose to "eat the forbidden fruit," you go into a state of consciousness where you lose the perspective of the Christ mind. You can no longer see that all life is one and that if you hurt another part of life, you are also hurting yourself. Instead, you now see through the filter of the death consciousness. This makes you believe you are a separate being, and thus you can get away with harming others without affecting yourself.

Evil does not have some absolute or objective existence. God did not allow evil on earth; we are the ones who continue to allow evil by remaining in the death consciousness. Evil is the result of a failure to see the reality of the Christ consciousness, namely the underlying oneness of all life. Jesus himself affirmed that oneness in both a vertical and horizontal way in the following quotes:

> I and my Father are one. (John 10:30)

> Verily I say unto you, Inasmuch as ye have done it unto one of the least of these my brethren, ye have done it unto me. (Matthew 25:40)

Jesus affirmed that when you see with the clarity of the Christ mind, you see that you are a spiritual being who came from a higher realm. You can indeed find the kingdom of God right within yourself. He also affirmed that when you see this vertical oneness, you see that all other people came from the same source. This makes you realize your oneness with all people. At that point, it becomes natural for you to live up to what according to Jesus is the most important point for being a Christian:

> Thou shalt love the Lord thy God with all thy heart, and with all thy soul, and with all thy strength, and with all thy mind; and thy neighbour as thyself. (Luke 10:27)

I have said that we can't truly accept Jesus if we see no connection between him and us. Likewise, we cannot fully love God if we see no connection between ourselves and God. The same holds true for loving other people. The connection between us is the Christ mind, the Christ consciousness.

When we attain this mindset, we no longer have to struggle to avoid sinning. It follows naturally from seeing who we are because it gives us the direct experience of what is enlightened self-interest. This is in stark contrast to the ego-based self-interest, which is what causes us to create a downward spiral that can entrap us for many lifetimes.

Reinstating reincarnation as part of Christianity

As I have said, we live in an age where the scientific mindset has taught us to look at cause and effect. When you look at the effect that some people are born into suffering, you simply cannot explain how God could be good and just.

As I have argued, reincarnation was very much part of early Christianity, possibly taught by Jesus to his disciples. The removal of reincarnation was a political decision, made by the Roman Catholic Church in the sixth century. To this day, no mainstream Christian church has been willing to go back and look at this decision, putting back in what Catholic Church fathers and Roman emperors took out. I think this ruins any chance of mainstream Christianity reaching today's spiritual people.

Several surveys have shown that between a quarter and a third of all Christians already believe in reincarnation. Why has no modern church dared to openly acknowledge reincarnation as an integral part of the Christian faith? The explanation is that no church has dared to question the standard model, thus making themselves slaves of the early church fathers and their political aims.

The immediate advantage of making reincarnation part of Christianity is its explanatory power. In the long run, reincarnation will also allow Christian churches to offer their members a gradual path leading towards a higher state of consciousness. Without such a path, I see that Christianity will continue to shrink, and the speed at which it loses members will only accelerate. The only question is whether the Christian faith needs to die before it can be reincarnated and receive a second chance at life.

❧

What Jesus came to do
was to re-establish the initiatic path
from the original mystery school.

13 | WHY DO PEOPLE LEAVE CHRISTIANITY?

Why are some people so angry with Christianity?

Let us take another look at the explanatory power of reincarnation. Have you ever stepped back and tried to look at the big picture, considering why people react so differently to religion? If we look at the modern, industrialized world, we can identify several typical reactions:

- A rather large group of people are indifferent towards religion. They might go to church once in a while, but they really have no interest in a deeper understanding of spiritual concepts. They are focused on living a good, material life, and they don't want to be bothered by a religion that demands anything from them.

- A growing group of people are agnostics, and they take the stand that it is impossible to know anything for sure about God or the spiritual aspects of life.

- A growing group of people are very angry with religion, and especially Christianity. There is a phenomenon called the New Atheists, and some people have written books that accuse religion of being the cause of all warfare and conflict. Why are they so angry with Christianity when there are plenty of other religions in the world?

- A shrinking group of people hold on to a traditional Christian faith. In many of these people, you can detect a growing frustration, almost desperation. However, if Christianity really is the only true religion, why the desperation, why the sense that Christianity is under threat?

- Some people – in some countries a growing group – have taken this desperation to the extreme of expecting that Jesus will return to earth in the near future, thereby validating their beliefs, taking them to heaven and sending all who disagree with them to hell.

- A rapidly growing number of people have given up on Christianity but have a clearly spiritual approach to life. They see life as a path leading towards a higher state of consciousness that will qualify them for entry into a higher realm. This is not caused by membership of an outer religion on earth; it is a product of the development of their state of consciousness.

If you take the traditional Christian model, you cannot easily explain such differences. If we have only one lifetime, why are some people indifferent towards salvation and why are others so angry with religion? Did God create someone to be so angry with religion that he or she is guaranteed to go to hell? Why would a good and just God do that?

The scientific materialist view isn't any better at explaining this. It can only say that our tendency to believe or disbelieve in religion is a product of our genes or our upbringing. If the latter is the case, how do you explain that in modern times, many people have been brought up in a religious home only to reject the faith of their parents?

For that matter, one of the major proponents of the new atheism claims that religious people are genetically predisposed to believe in the illusion of a God. If you take that claim to its logical conclusion, all of our beliefs are the products of our genetic predisposition. Which would mean that atheists are genetically predisposed to reject religion.

This, of course, renders the stand taken by these atheists completely futile. They are telling religious people to go against their genetic predisposition (which according to their own claims is impossible) and accept that atheism is not simply a genetic predisposition but a higher reality. If everything is a product of genes and if all beliefs are produced in the physical brain, then there is no higher reality and no meaning in having any discussion at all. The New Atheists are contradicting themselves by saying that their genetic disposition makes them see an absolute truth whereas religious people's genes make them believe in an illusion. They are engaging in a rather immature game of telling religious people: "My genes are better than your genes."

How reincarnation explains different beliefs

Let us look at what reincarnation can say about why people have these different reactions to religion. The basic idea of reincarnation is, of course, that a human being is a soul that does not die when the physical body dies. The soul can reincarnate many times, and we take with us from lifetime to lifetime both the lessons we have learned and the psychological problems we have not resolved. Most of us are not consciously aware of this, but the influence from past lives comes through the subconscious mind.

By the way, there is extensive literature documenting thousands of cases where children have remembered their last lifetimes, often being able to give verifiable details that they simply could not have learned in this lifetime. There are also books about people who have been hypnotically regressed or who have spontaneously remembered past lives. Numerous near-death experiences also confirm the reality of reincarnation and the soul's survival of physical death.

Christianity has been in existence for 2,000 years, which means that in the modern world we might have a large number of souls who have had several embodiments in which they were exposed to mainstream Christianity. This exposure might have left a lasting impact on these souls, which can explain the attitude towards Christianity that they display in this lifetime. Let us look at some possible scenarios:

- A basic aspect of reincarnation is the idea that when a soul first incarnates on earth, it is very focused on the physical, material aspects of life. This can explain why many people are indifferent towards religion or spirituality. There is a completely natural phase in which a soul is meant to focus on the material aspects of life, including learning how to use the physical body or how to create a good material life for itself. In the modern industrial part of the world, we have many souls who have attained some mastery of this, but they have not yet crossed the line where they are ready to consider a deeper, meaning a more spiritual, purpose to life.

• Some souls have in several past lifetimes been directly exposed to the violent aspects of the Christian faith. They might have been killed by Christians, for example in the crusades or the witch hunts, and this created psychological wounds in the souls that they have not yet healed. On the other hand, they might also have been crusaders or in other ways have fought on the side of Christianity. They might have realized this is not in accordance with Jesus' true teachings, deeply regretting having been fooled into thinking it was justifiable to kill or torture other human beings. Both scenarios would explain why these souls are very angry with Christianity and why they accuse Christianity of being the source of violence and war. It also explains why they are so intent on proving mainstream Christianity wrong. We might say that such souls are more advanced than the materially focused souls, yet they have not yet come to the maturity where they can take full responsibility for themselves. Of course, religion is not the cause of warfare: unresolved human psychology is.

• Some souls have had several lifetimes in which they were born into a Christian culture. They lived those lifetimes firmly believing in the official model of salvation, and each time they expected to be saved after they died. After they had several experiences of being sent back to earth, their souls retained the memory that the standard Christian model cannot fulfill its promise of salvation. They have now come into embodiment with an inner soul knowing that the standard view of salvation simply does not work. As a result, some of them might be very angry with Christianity, or they may be so confused that they simply don't know what to believe. On the one hand, they have some inner memory that there is life after death, but they cannot see this reflected in the Christian religion so they are stuck in a no-god's land.

• Other souls have not yet come to the realization that the standard model promises an impossible salvation. They are again born into the Christian religion, and they have the feeling that they must hold on to it against all challenges. Instead of acknowledging their frustration, they seek to ignore or deny it as best they can, clinging to the belief that membership of the outer religion will save them.

• Some souls might in past lives have used the Christian religion to build a sense that because they were good Christians, they were superior to other people. If they are not yet ready to give up this superiority (accepting the call of Jesus to love their neighbors as themselves), they will not be willing to admit that Christianity could be wrong. If their Christian beliefs were proven wrong, they themselves would be wrong and their sense of superiority would evaporate. You can see this psychological mechanism in how the scribes, the Pharisees and the Sanhedrin attacked Jesus when he challenged their sense of superiority. Such souls cling to the belief that any day Jesus will return and validate their superiority.

• Some people have indeed been disappointed by official Christianity in past lifetimes, but they have passed through the stage of being angry or confused. Instead, they have reached a higher level of soul maturity where they have taken responsibility for their own state of consciousness. They have looked for a form of spirituality that offers them a systematic path. So far, many of these souls have not found that path in Christianity, but I believe many of them could benefit from coming to see Jesus as a unique teacher of this inner path of initiation. If enough of these people would acknowledge that Jesus is by no means obsolete, it might even have a positive impact on transforming Christianity.

There are some experiences
we cannot have if we retain the
awareness that we are connected
to other beings.

14 | WHAT IS CHRIST AND ANTI-CHRIST?

The unasked question

I have said that there are many questions that the standard model cannot answer. There are also questions that the standard model cannot even ask. One such question is this: What exactly is Christ? Let us take another look at this quote from John, Chapter 1:

> 1 In the beginning was the Word, and the Word was with God, and the Word was God.
> 2 The same was in the beginning with God.
> 3 All things were made by him; and without him was not any thing made that was made.

I have argued that "Word" is better translated as "Logos," and that this is the basic principle used by God to design everything in creation. We can therefore see that "Christ" cannot be understood fully by saying it is referring to a historical human being appearing here on this little planet. Christ must be something beyond any particular form because it is the source of all form.

I have argued that Christ is a universal form of consciousness, meaning that everything was created from the Christ consciousness or Christ principle. To explain this in greater depth, we need to again consider whether God is stupid. What was going through God's mind as he contemplated creating self-aware beings (us) and giving them free will?

God must have been able to foresee that by giving us free will, it became possible that we could choose to descend into the death consciousness. God would then have faced the question of how we could ever get out of the death consciousness. Obviously, by giving us free will, God made it impossible for himself to "force" us out of the death consciousness. We would have to get out of it the same way we got into it, namely through our own choices.

By creating the Christ consciousness as the firstborn son and then creating everything else from that consciousness, God had already provided the solution. We can go into the death consciousness and we can forget that we are spiritual beings, but we can never lose our longing for something beyond the death consciousness. We can never be fully satisfied by what the death consciousness offers us. There will come a point when we have had enough of the experiences that the death consciousness offers us and we want more.

On top of that, the Christ consciousness provides us a systematic path that can lead us – step by step – out of the death consciousness. We can never lose this ability to climb back out of the death consciousness. The universal Christ consciousness is the door that no man can shut.

As I said, Christ has two aspects, the universal and the individualized. The universal Christ consciousness is the unifying principle behind all of the many forms we see in the world.

Behind every form, no matter how low or hellish it might seem to us, there is the universal Christ consciousness. If we can train our minds to see beyond the outer form – following Jesus' call to stop judging after appearances – we can come to see the underlying oneness behind all diversified forms. This is when Christ has become individualized or has taken incarnation in us. The conclusion is that Christ means oneness.

What is anti-christ?

Another question that the standard model does not ask is: What exactly is anti-christ? It is assumed that as Christ is the person of Jesus, anti-christ is a devil, a real being that is supposedly opposing God. Yet if God is almighty, how can anything oppose or threaten God? Where did the devil come from? If everything is created by God, does that mean God created the devil? Does that mean the devil is somehow necessary in creation?

Some of the early Gnostics actually claimed that there was a polarity between God and a demiurge that opposed God. The world is locked in a titanic struggle between these two opposing forces, and it is an uncertainty who will win. This is reflected in the standard model that portrays the devil as a real being who has the power to force souls into hell. Jesus or Christ is supposedly come to destroy the devil and save all souls from going to hell.

We can now propose an alternative view. In its broadest sense, anti-christ is a state of consciousness that is the opposite of Christ. Christ is oneness, meaning that anti-christ is separation.

As we have seen, the Christ consciousness is the underlying principle from which everything is created. The deeper meaning is that – in reality – everything is one. There never has been and never can be anything that is truly separated from the Christ consciousness. Because the Christ consciousness is always one with God, nothing can be separated from God in reality. This means that the devil is not a real being that exists as the opposite polarity of God and is locked in a struggle with God. God is all there is and in God there are no divisions. Therefore, nothing can oppose God.

How come we can experience that we are separated from God and separated from each other? Take note that we are *experiencing* division, meaning that division exists only in the mind. Division and separation are illusions that are created by a specific state of consciousness, namely anti-christ.

Division and separation are not real. This means that anti-christ is not real. The Christ does not come to save us from a devil that is real. The Christ comes to save us from the illusion that separation is real.

What does it mean to truly accept Christ? It means to accept that oneness is real and separation is unreal. Accepting Christ means freeing our minds from the illusion of separation so we can see the underlying truth that oneness is the only reality. Jesus came to show us that we all have the potential to overcome the illusion of separation and rise to a higher level of consciousness than the consciousness of death. In this consciousness of life, we have a direct experience of the oneness of all life. We are seeing life through the reality of oneness rather than seeing through the filter of separation.

Jesus did not come to save us from a devil that is a real force outside of us. Jesus came to save us from a devil that is inside our own minds, the devil that makes separation seem real. Entering the kingdom of God that is within us means coming to the direct experience that the Christ mind is already within us and is simply awaiting our permission to express itself through us. The universal Christ mind is waiting to "take incarnation" through our individual minds.

Jesus came to save us from an illusion, the illusion that we are separated from God's kingdom by a barrier that we did not create and thus cannot overcome by our internal powers. We follow Christ by giving up the separate sense of identity, the separate life, and being reborn into a new life of oneness.

What is the devil inside of us?

How would Jesus have explained what I just said to people who knew what people knew 2,000 years ago? Do we have better options for explaining this today? I think we do, and the key is the concept of the ego. The ego is the devil inside of us, it is created from the consciousness of separation, the mind of anti-christ. The ego has one function and one function only: to make it seem real that we are separate beings. We are separated from God and from each other.

We first descended to earth a long time ago, and at one point in time we made the decision to accept the illusion of separation. Why did we do this? We might have done it as a reaction to other beings who were already in separation and who attacked us, seeking to force us to oppose them. We might have done it in order to experience what it is like to be a separate being.

There are some experiences we cannot have if we retain the awareness that we are connected to other beings. One of Jesus' most famous statements is obviously: Do unto others as you want them to do to you. What would it actually take to live that statement? Would it not take that you overcome the illusion of separation so you see that because we are all one, what you do to another human being, you are also doing to yourself?

If you look at the world, it is not hard to see that many people are very much attached to the kind of experiences you can have only as a separate being. How can you have the experience of being a powerful warrior if you realize that by killing others you are killing part of yourself? How can you experience being better than others when you realize we are all one? When you see the reality of oneness, many human endeavors suddenly become the "vanities of vanity, all is vanity." Some might not want to give up certain human activities.

Has Christianity shut out Christ?

I earlier talked about the possibility that human beings are at different levels of awareness. We can now define another consideration: How deeply have people gone into separation or how close have they come to oneness? We can even say that because God has given us free will, and therefore has given us the option to go into separation, it is perfectly acceptable that some people still have not had enough of the kind of experiences we can have only through separation.

These are the kind of people who might be ready for Jesus' outer teachings. For example, some still have a need for feeling that they belong to the only true religion and that this membership makes them better in the eyes of God than all other people. I have no problem with mainstream Christianity catering to the needs of such people.

I do have a problem when mainstream Christianity claims that it is the only form of Christianity. The fact that so many people have left Christianity is to me proof that in this age more and more people have had enough of the experiences we have through separation. They are ready to enter the path of oneness, and Jesus came to offer that path to those who are ready. Therefore, I object to the undeniable fact that mainstream Christianity still seeks to deny this path to everyone. How can an institution on earth claim to represent Christ and at the same time attempt to shut Christ out of this world? Is it any wonder that it cannot meet the psycho-spiritual needs of todays more mature spiritual seekers?

Are Christians denying Christ?

We now see a very interesting conclusion. Christ is the principle of oneness whereas anti-christ is the denial of oneness, the denial of Christ.

Jesus did not come to save us by doing something for us that we cannot do for ourselves. He came to awaken us from the illusion of separation by showing us that we do have access to the Christ consciousness within ourselves. We don't need an external church or power elite in order to access Christ. He resides in the kingdom within us.

Take note of a subtle distinction. Many Christians will say that what I teach here is the works of the devil because I am the one denying Christ by saying that we don't need Jesus in order to be saved. Yet that is not what I am saying.

When you have become blinded by the death consciousness, your mind is – as far as it sees itself – a separate mind. There is a hint at this in the Genesis story of the fall of Adam and Eve. God had supposedly told them that if they ate of the fruit of the knowledge of good and evil, they would surely die. The serpent makes them doubt this by saying they will not *"surely"* die. They then eat the fruit and they don't die but are cast out of paradise. Does that mean God lied to Adam and Eve?

When you begin to understand what Jesus meant when he talked about death, you gain a deeper understanding. As I have said, Jesus did not talk about physical death but a spiritual or psychological death. What Jesus called life is a state of consciousness in which we see ourselves as one with or at least connected to God and all life. What Jesus called death is a state of consciousness in which we see ourselves separated from God and all life.

Right now you have a certain sense of identity. Before Adam and Eve ate the forbidden fruit, they had a sense of identity of being connected to God, or rather to their spiritual teacher. When they partook of the consciousness of anti-christ, the consciousness of separation, that sense of identity did indeed die. Adam and Eve were then reborn into a new identity in which they saw themselves as separate beings. Because of the nature of separation, they did not remember their former state and thus did not realize it had died.

Once we are trapped in the consciousness of death, there literally is no way out. The main characteristic of the mind of anti-christ is that once you are in it, you cannot see beyond it. As Albert Einstein said: "You cannot solve a problem with the same state of consciousness that created the problem." Once we have eaten of the fruit of separation, there is no way we can use the consciousness of separation to get back to oneness.

How can people then be saved from the consciousness of death? Only when the Christ comes and offers them the consciousness of life. This is where it is necessary to make a subtle distinction. In reality, the Christ does not appear from outside yourself because the Christ is already within you. Yet when you are trapped in the consciousness of separation, you cannot see that Christ is within you. Thus, when the Christ does appear, you will *perceive* that the Christ is coming to you from the outside. Because you are in separation, you will think that the Christ can come to you only as an external source. This is indeed why mainstream Christianity was successful in creating the idol of Jesus as the exclusive incarnation of the Christ consciousness—past, present or future. In reality, Jesus came to demonstrate that all of us have the potential to become the incarnation of Christ, and we do so by overcoming the illusion that we are separated from Christ, that Christ is not within us.

My conclusion is that most of the people who claim to be "good Christians" and see themselves as the true followers of Jesus are actually engaged in a very deceptive game created by the mind of anti-christ. It is the game of projecting that the Christ is outside yourself, thereby denying the reality that you will never find Christ as long as you are looking for him outside yourself. You will find Christ only when you stop looking for him outside and look for him the only place he can be found, namely within you.

In my view, mainstream Christian churches are denying the central reality that Jesus came to give us, namely that the Christ is within everyone. As I have said, in order to have the experience that you are a separate being, you will have to deny this reality. Since God has given all people free will, I champion people's right to have that experience for as long as they want. I just wonder how many Christians would actually continue going to their respective churches if they truly understood that those churches have, for over 1600 years, reinforced the denial of Christ on this planet? This, of course, brings up an even more provocative question.

Is Christianity Satanism in disguise?

I know that even verbalizing this question will cause many Christians to reject this book, but I am not writing for such people. I am writing for those who are ready to consider the questions that the mainstream model cannot even formulate. Let us consider the question: "What exactly is Satan?" How did

Jesus define Satan? Let us begin by looking at what is surely one of the most baffling passages in the New Testament:

> 13 When Jesus came into the coasts of Caesarea Philippi, he asked his disciples, saying, Whom do men say that I the Son of man am?
> 14 And they said, Some say that thou art John the Baptist: some, Elias; and others, Jeremias, or one of the prophets.
> 15 He saith unto them, But whom say ye that I am?
> 16 And Simon Peter answered and said, Thou art the Christ, the Son of the living God.
> 17 And Jesus answered and said unto him, Blessed art thou, Simon Barjona: for flesh and blood hath not revealed it unto thee, but my Father which is in heaven.
> 18 And I say also unto thee, That thou art Peter, and upon this rock I will build my church; and the gates of hell shall not prevail against it.
>
> 21 From that time forth began Jesus to shew unto his disciples, how that he must go unto Jerusalem, and suffer many things of the elders and chief priests and scribes, and be killed, and be raised again the third day.
> 22 Then Peter took him, and began to rebuke him, saying, Be it far from thee, Lord: this shall not be unto thee.
> 23 But he turned, and said unto Peter, Get thee behind me, Satan: thou art an offence unto me: for thou savourest not the things that be of God, but those that be of men.
> 24 Then said Jesus unto his disciples, If any man will come after me, let him deny himself, and take up his cross, and follow me.
> 25 For whosoever will save his life shall lose it: and whosoever will lose his life for my sake shall find it.
> (Matthew, Chapter 16)

I have deliberately divided this passage into two distinct parts. In the first part, Jesus tells Peter that he is the rock upon which he will build his church. In the second part, Jesus tells Peter that he is Satan. Was Jesus schizophrenic or is there a deeper meaning?

The key statement in the first passage is this: "flesh and blood hath not revealed it unto thee, but my Father which is in heaven." This symbolizes the fact that because the Christ consciousness is in everything, we all have the potential to recognize Christ. Even when we are still in the death consciousness and see ourselves as separate beings, we have the capacity to recognize that a person or idea is coming from a distinctly higher level of consciousness than our own. What Jesus is saying here is not that the person of Peter is the rock upon which he will build his church. In reality, he is saying that he will build his church on the ability to recognize a higher state of consciousness, an ability all of us have if we are willing to use it. This ability is what we earlier called the key of knowledge.

The key statement in the second passage is: "thou savourest not the things that be of God, but those that be of men." The situation is that Jesus is telling his disciples what will happen with his crucifixion and death. This does not fit into the human expectations, the mental image, that Peter has for what should happen to the Christ, the son of the Living God. Peter therefore takes the step of seeking to force or manipulate Jesus into denying his true mission and instead conforming to Peter's vision based on the things that be of men. Jesus affirms that as the individualized Christ, he intends to behave according to the things that be of God.

The consciousness represented by the "fruit of the knowledge of good and evil" is a state of consciousness that believes it is like a god on earth. Therefore, it has the capacity and right to define what is good and evil true and false, right and wrong.

It believes that it knows better than God how the universe should work, and that is precisely why it is impossible for us to get out of the death consciousness by using the death consciousness. Trying to do this will only lead us deeper and deeper into the illusions of anti-christ and make us more convinced that the illusions are reality.

The only way out is to use our ability to recognize something that comes from outside the consciousness of anti-christ, namely something or someone that represents the Christ consciousness. The crucial distinction is that it is not enough to recognize this once. It is a continuos process where we constantly reach for the truth of Christ and use it to see through the illusions of our present frame of mind. This is what Jesus meant by saying that if we want to follow him, we must deny our separate selves, take up our crosses – a symbol for the path of transcending the separate self – and follow the Christ wherever he takes us.

The true path delivered by Jesus is an ongoing process of letting the separate self die so that we are reborn into a higher sense of self that is closer to oneness. That is why Paul said: "I die daily." The central element of this path is that we constantly use any impulse from the Christ consciousness to climb above the consciousness of separation. We do not take an impulse from the Christ consciousness and seek to force it into the mental box of the separate self, thereby seeking to get Christ to validate and affirm the illusions of anti-christ.

Why do I say that Christianity is a disguised form of Satanism? In its broadest form, Satan is the state of consciousness that seeks to force the Christ (the things that be of God) to validate the illusions of anti-christ (the things that be of men).

Since the very beginning, most people have not understood what it really means to follow Christ. They have not been able to grasp that it means to rise to a state of consciousness that

14 | What Is Christ and Anti-Christ?

is so much higher, so fundamentally different, from what we call normal human awareness. This is not to blame anyone, for it truly is not easy to grasp the Christ consciousness, let alone to be one with it. This is demonstrated by the fact that even Jesus' own disciples did not get his true message. Peter himself denied Jesus three times, thus continuing in the denial of the necessity to follow Christ by denying his human self.

The Catholic Church claims to base its authority on a direct succession of Popes from Peter to the present. I think what the Catholic Church is based on is not the authority of Peter but the consciousness of Peter. This is the consciousness that refuses to let the separate self die but instead reinterprets the Word of Christ so it seemingly confirms the "things that be of men," the illusions of anti-christ.

This consciousness was part of Christianity from the beginning. As I have argued, Jesus meant to form a movement where people would continually receive new revelation from the comforter, the Holy Spirit. The purpose was to make sure that the Christian movement would never solidify into dogmas and doctrines that sprang from the human consciousness.

In the first couple of centuries, there was a tension between people who followed the mystical path and those who wanted to form a unified and codified church. This process became accelerated and institutionalized with the formation of the Catholic Church. For over a thousand years, the leaders of the Catholic Church used the words of Christ, now confined to the existing scriptures and no longer the Living Word, to validate and conform man-made beliefs and desires. They created the exact kind of church that Jesus denounced and whose leaders had him executed.

What modern church has been willing to air the dirty laundry of Christianity's past and make use of the comforter to correct past errors. Therefore, those who have not done so are upholding the very consciousness that took over the Christian religion. That consciousness is what Jesus himself called Satan. From this perspective, Christianity is indeed Satanism in disguise.

15 | WHAT IS TRUTH?

Following Christ—again and again

Saying that Christianity is a camouflaged form of Satanism is, of course, a radical statement. But is it true? What about the many sincere and well-meaning Christians who are doing everything they can to be kind to others and do good works? Are they not doing what Jesus wants them to do as best they are able to see it?

The key words in the previous sentence are: "as best they are able to see it." The key question is: "Is what most Christians see the same that Jesus wants them to see?" As I have argued, it isn't because Christianity has almost turned Jesus' teaching on its head.

The standard model presents salvation as an either-or proposition. You either qualify or you don't. In order to be saved, you have to accept Christ and that means becoming a member of the only true Christian church. Once you have done so, the rest is just a matter of believing a set of doctrines and following a set of rules defined by your church. The form of salvation that Jesus gave us is a gradual path of raising our consciousness to a level that is radically different from the death consciousness.

I have argued that following the way of Christ is a gradual process. We have, over many lifetimes, accepted a large number of illusions that spring from the mind of anti-christ. These are deposited in our subconscious minds, and our egos use them to prevent us from knowing the reality that Jesus came to show us. None of us can overcome all of these illusions in one giant step. If we did, we would lose our sense of identity and continuity and go through an identity crisis.

The way of Jesus does not require us to let go of all illusions in one step. It requires us to overcome one illusion at a time and to continue doing so for the rest of our lives. According to the standard model, Christ comes to you once and if you accept him, you are saved. According to the Way of Jesus, Christ comes to you over and over again, each time in order to offer you an alternative to one of your illusions.

You might face the choice to accept or reject Christ millions of times during a lifetime. I would argue that if you think it is enough to accept Christ once and then follow the rules of an outer church, you may have accepted Christ that one time, but then you have rejected him ever since.

When we accept Christ, we can only do so based on the state of consciousness we have at that time. That state of consciousness is colored by a lot of illusions so our concept of what it means to accept Christ is incomplete. It is our challenge to continue to accept that Christ will appear to us again and again, every time in order to challenge another illusion. It is only by being willing to let part of the human self die every day that we truly follow Christ. This is the initiation Peter failed and that is why Jesus said to him: "Get thee behind me, Satan."

How can we know truth?

We can now adopt a sense of humility and acknowledge something very profound: All of us have an ego and we will *never* know truth through that human self. When we think that what the ego sees as truth really is truth, we reject Christ. That is precisely what the ego, the prince of this world or Satan wants us to do.

Then what is Christ truth? How can we ever know what is right? Let us take a look at an interesting passage from when Jesus was brought to trial in front of Pontius Pilate:

> 37 Pilate therefore said unto him, Art thou a king then? Jesus answered, Thou sayest that I am a king. To this end was I born, and for this cause came I into the world, that I should bear witness unto the truth. Every one that is of the truth heareth my voice.
> 38 Pilate saith unto him, What is truth? (John, Chapter 18)

Pilate expresses the frustration felt by many people in the modern world. Many of those who have left Christianity have done so because they can no longer believe in the "truth" presented by the standard model. Neither can they believe in the "truth" presented by science that we are evolved monkeys. If we can turn to neither Christianity nor science, then where can we turn? Isn't there something that is true in this world?

Since before the time of Jesus, philosophers have debated the very question of how we can know truth. There are two main schools of philosophy, the rationalist and the empiricists.

The rationalists say that we can know truth by using the reasoning faculties of the mind, and the empiricists say we can know truth only through direct experience.

Who is right? What if none of them are right? What if there is an alternative view of truth. Consider one of Jesus' more enigmatic statements:

> Jesus saith unto him, I am the way, the truth, and the life: no man cometh unto the Father, but by me. (John, 14:6)

Christians have used this as one of the main arguments that proves Christianity is the only true religion. Did Jesus say that an outer religion was the "way, the truth and the life?" He did not; he said: "I am." Christians have argued that Jesus as a historical person is the way, the truth and the life because he was the only son of God. This brings us back to the question of whether anyone was saved before Jesus took embodiment on earth.

The way out of this dilemma is to reach back to what I said earlier. The real way, truth and life is the Universal Christ consciousness. This consciousness cannot express itself directly in this world, but can do so only through an individual who has attained oneness with it. What this statement truly means is: "I, the universal Christ consciousness, am the way, the truth and the life. No man comes to the father except by attaining oneness with me, thereby becoming the individualized Christ incarnate."

How can we know truth? We can now see something truly profound and liberating. We can *never* know truth through the faculties of the separate mind, the separate self. We can know truth *only* through the Christ consciousness. Yet this presents a unique challenge. The Christ consciousness is *not* something we can know from a distance.

When we normally think of knowing something, we see it as a process whereby we, as a separate subject, study a remote object. What Jesus and the Christ consciousness calls us to do is to transcend this approach to achieving knowledge. Instead, we are called to stop thinking we can know Christ from a distance. We are called to overcome the subject-object barrier and come into oneness – gnosis – with the Christ consciousness. Only when we let that mind be in us which was also in Christ Jesus will we know truth.

Being as gods knowing good and evil

This, of course, brings up a very difficult question. Is any of the knowledge found in this world true in an ultimate sense? Let me approach that question by referring to another enigmatic statement made by Jesus (who really is a master of Zen koans):

> 34 Think not that I am come to send peace on earth: I came not to send peace, but a sword.
> 35 For I am come to set a man at variance against his father, and the daughter against her mother, and the daughter in law against her mother in law.
> 36 And a man's foes shall be they of his own household.
> (Matthew, Chapter 10)

I have not yet heard a Christian minister who could make sense of this statement, but I think we can get far by using what we discussed earlier. According to Jesus, we human beings are trapped in the death consciousness, and we are blinded by the illusions of anti-christ. Jesus has come to awaken us from that state by offering us the life of the Christ consciousness. How exactly is he doing this?

In order to understand this, we have to take a look at the main characteristic of the death consciousness. This means we need to take another look at Genesis and the situation where the serpent is tempting Eve. As mentioned earlier, Adam and Eve had been told that they were not allowed to eat of the fruit of the tree of the knowledge of good and evil, and if they did, they would surely die. Here is what the serpent said:

> 4 And the serpent said unto the woman, Ye shall not surely die:
> 5 For God doth know that in the day ye eat thereof, then your eyes shall be opened, and ye shall be as gods, knowing good and evil. (Genesis, Chapter 3)

The central words here are: "ye shall be as gods, knowing good and evil." What exactly does this mean? Take the fact that Jesus – who had come to set people free from the death consciousness – was constantly opposed by religious people who had a very specific approach to truth. The scribes and Pharisees used the words of the Old Testament to reason that Jesus could not be the Messiah. Based on their reasoning, they felt fully justified in not only rejecting him but in killing him.

Consider the expression that people "are playing God." It often refers to the fact that when people feel that they can decide whether another human being should live or die, then they are taking upon themselves the power of God.

We now see that what the serpent said to Eve was a very subtle deception. The deeper meaning is that when you eat the fruit of the knowledge of good and evil, you enter into a specific state of consciousness. In this state of consciousness, you think that you – as a separate individual – have the right and the power to define what is truth, to define what is good and evil in an ultimate sense. You also think that you have a right to impose your definition upon others, even that you have a right to kill them if they will not accept your "truth" over their own.

The main characteristic of the death consciousness is that it causes people to define many different "truths." Each group believes that their truth is the only absolute one and that all of the others are of the devil. Therefore, they feel justified in seeking to impose their "truth" upon others, even killing those who will not comply.

What exactly killed Jesus?

When the scribes and Pharisees attacked Jesus, they felt that they had the superior truth and that what Jesus said was a lie and came from the devil. In doing this, they had set themselves up as gods on earth, deciding what was good and evil and deciding whether the embodied Christ should live or die. They failed the initiation of Christ and sought to get Jesus to conform to their "truth." When Jesus would not conform, they were willing to kill him in order to silence the threat to their "truth." What did Jesus say to these people?

> Ye are of your father the devil, and the lusts of your father ye will do. He was a murderer from the beginning, and abode not in the truth, because there is no truth in him. When he speaketh a lie, he speaketh of his own: for he is a liar, and the father of it. (John 8:44)

The devil is, in its most universal sense, the consciousness of anti-christ, the consciousness of separation. The consciousness of Christ is the consciousness of oneness. How do you separate from oneness? You create the illusion that oneness can be divided into separate parts that are opposing each other. Once you have this division, you uphold it as the only reality, meaning you have now obscured (in the minds of those who have partaken of the lie) the underlying oneness of all life. The most basic division of all is good and evil. They are fundamental opposites that are locked in an epic struggle to attain supremacy by destroying the opposite.

We now see the most profound realization that Jesus wanted to give to his true disciples. Both good and evil are defined by the consciousness of anti-christ, meaning that both of them are separated from the indivisible truth of Christ!

What killed Jesus? It was the consciousness of the devil. It is the father of lies because it gave rise to the illusion that reality or oneness can be divided into two opposites, one of which must destroy the other. It was a murderer from the beginning because in order to make the illusion of separation believable, it had to murder oneness, it had to murder the Christ. That is why the consciousness of the devil had to murder Christ when he appeared in an individualized form.

Who was it that murdered Christ? It was the people who had embodied, individualized, the universal consciousness of anti-christ. They thought they were as gods on earth, and when the embodied Christ challenged them, they were not willing to give up that feeling of superiority. They did the lusts of their father and murdered the embodied Christ.

Unfortunately for them, Jesus wasn't so easy to kill. Therefore, the universal consciousness of the devil now had to implement a second part of its strategy, namely to make sure that no one would dare to follow Jesus' example and likewise embody the Christ consciousness. The devil was thwarted by the fact that Jesus dared to embody the Christ consciousness, and he wanted to make sure that no one else would dare to follow Jesus' example and become the Christ in embodiment.

How was this goal accomplished? The universal consciousness of anti-christ used those who had individualized itself. People with the exact same mindset as the scribes and Pharisees entered the Christian religion, and they then served to kill the example of Jesus. They did this by creating an organization that claims to have the power of being as a god on earth, defining what is good and what is evil, what is Christ and what is not.

If you accept reincarnation, you can speculate that the very same souls who had Jesus physically murdered later embodied as leaders of the Christian movement and then murdered Jesus' example. You might even speculate that some of these souls have continued to embody and are found in the leadership of Christian churches today. How else do you explain that those churches are upholding the murder of the Christ in the rest of us?

The Word and words

How does the devil accomplish the feat of murdering truth? He simply projects the idea that truth can be captured in words. Take a look at the opening of the Gospel of John:

> In the beginning was the Word, and the Word was with God, and the Word was God.

As mentioned, "the Word" can also be translated as "Logos," which represents the indivisible oneness of all. There is a fundamental difference between "the Word" and "words." The Word indicates oneness whereas we use words to set things apart from each other. The word "table" refers to a thing that is clearly set apart from another thing called "chair."

If I say "Yes," you can say "No." If I say "true," you can say "false." If I say "good," you can say "evil." If I say "God exists," you can say "There is no God." We now see a fundamental reality: Any statement made with words can be contradicted by another statement made by words. Ultimate, indivisible truth can never be captured in words.

It now becomes clear how the devil has managed to divide us. He has – through the serpent – made us believe that we are as gods on earth. We have the right to define a certain statement with words and then to declare that this statement is the infallible and absolute truth, even that it is "the word of God." In our hubris of thinking we are gods, we now believe that it is our duty to defeat the devil by getting all people to accept our worded statement as infallible, even killing those who refuse to comply.

I earlier said that it truly is amazing how the non-violent teachings of Jesus could be used to create a religion that precipitated the Crusades, the Inquisition, the witch hunts, the persecution of scientists and other atrocities. We can now see why this happened. The stark reality is that Christianity was taken over by the very same mindset that caused people to kill Christ. The leaders of the Christian religion started thinking they were as gods on earth and that they had the right to define what is truth and whether the Christ in all should live or die.

How did Jesus use words?

The standard Christian model takes a very specific approach to the concept of truth. It has taken – hook, line and sinker – the devil's bait that truth can be defined in words. It assumes that Jesus represented truth, and thus he came to give us truth by giving us worded statements. Those statements were recorded accurately in the Bible, meaning that if you read the worded statements in the Bible, you have the absolute and infallible truth.

15 | What Is Truth?

If this were indeed true, then how do we explain that there are over 20,000 Christian churches and sects and that they are divided precisely because they look at the very same words in the Bible and come up with different interpretations? If the words in the Bible were the infallible Word of God – if they were "The Word" – they should not give rise to division. Since Christians themselves have proven so abundantly that the words in the Bible do give rise to division, we must conclude that the Bible is not the infallible Word of God because "The Word" cannot be captured in and confined to the words we use here on earth. If we really want to know truth, we have to go beyond words and reach for "The Word."

We now see that Jesus faced a very difficult challenge. As I have said, the universal Christ consciousness can express itself in this world only when individualized. The embodied Christ has to speak to us in words; there is simply no other way. The real question is whether we take what the embodied Christ says and interprets the words through the consciousness of anti-christ – the consciousness of separation and division – or whether wee seek to use the words only as a tool for reaching for the consciousness of Christ, the consciousness of oneness. Are Christians using Jesus' words to help the cause of the devil, which is to keep us divided? Or are they using Jesus' words to further the cause of Christ, which is to help us escape separateness and embrace oneness?

Jesus – and certainly the universal Christ mind – knew the problem with words. Jesus had to say *something* in order to awaken us. He did everything possible to prevent us from going into the consciousness of the scribes and Pharisees and interpret his words through their definition of good and evil. He attempted to give us many seemingly contradictory or enigmatic statements in order to shake us out of our normal way of thinking. Yet he probably knew that this would not work for all people, so what was his Plan B?

The inevitable consequence of giving us words

What might Jesus have meant when he said: "I am come to set a man at variance against his father...?" What if he meant that he knew exactly how some people would use his words? I have mentioned that the goal of the path of Christhood is that you – as an embodied individual – attain oneness with the universal Christ mind. Jesus attained this, meaning that the Christ mind could speak through him and make direct statements. Some of Jesus' statements were not actually referring to him as a historical person. The statement "I am the way, the truth and the life" did not refer to Jesus as a person. It was the Universal Christ consciousness speaking through him and speaking about itself.

Part of Jesus' mission was to allow the universal Christ mind to speak through him because it is the flow of Spirit that has the power and authority to awaken people. Jesus knew that by allowing this, he would force people to react in one of three ways:

- Some people would see his "I am" statements as crazy and use it as an excuse for rejecting him. They would think no person could embody the Christ consciousness.

- Some would accept him as the Christ but would interpret his "I am" statements literally. They would believe it referred to him as a historical person. They would think he was the fullness of the Christ consciousness.

- Some would accept that one person can embody the Christ consciousness and that Jesus did so. They would also see that no person can embody the fullness of the universal Christ mind. Therefore, they would be inspired by Jesus' example to allow the universal Christ mind to take embodiment through them also.

Those who chose option one and two would do so because they were still trapped in the illusion of separation. Those who chose option two would take the appearance of the Christ in Jesus and use it to reinforce separation by turning Jesus' words and actions into another religion that claims to be the only true one. They would turn Christianity into the exact same type of religion as the Jewish religion whose leaders killed Christ. By doing so they would inevitably set themselves and Christianity in conflict against all who did not accept the choice they had made.

This is exactly what we have seen. The people who chose option two started forming a centralized church, and in the beginning it saw itself in opposition to the Gnostics. It then became the Roman Catholic Church and now saw itself in opposition to everyone else. This led to the split between the Eastern Church and the Western Church in the Aryan controversy. It led to the suppression of the teachings of the Greek philosophers and any other teaching that contradicted the one, infallible doctrine. It led to the massacre of the Cathars, the Crusades, the inquisition, the witch hunts, the persecution of early scientists. It even led to the split in Christianity itself, first with Lutheranism and then with numerous other churches and sects. When will Christianity finally have fractured so much that people see the absurdity of interpreting the words of Jesus through the filter of the separate mind? When will people reach for the Christ mind and reach for the consciousness of oneness? Perhaps Jesus knew exactly that this would be the result? Perhaps he deliberately provoked those in the consciousness of separation to take his words and turn them into another religion that only promoted division by claiming that it has the absolute truth? What could be Jesus' purpose for doing so? If we accept reincarnation, we can gain a different perspective.

Perhaps Jesus knew that many souls could not rise above the illusions of anti-christ in just one lifetime. He also knew that many souls were so blinded by these illusions that they did not have ears to hear what he was truly saying about oneness. In order to speed up their process of growth, he gave them the justification for creating another religion that would promote division. The purpose was to reinforce the tendency to fight until people had taken it to such an extreme that they began to clearly see the discrepancy between their violent behavior and the non-violent words and example of Christ.

How do we explain that so many people in the modern world have started seeing the complete fallacy of Christianity's violent past? How come so many have started to see the fallacy of Christianity's approach to truth? Is it perhaps because some of us have now matured to the point where we are ready to leave behind the consciousness of separation and begin to truly embrace the Spirit of Oneness? We now see that Jesus might have had a dual purpose for making the following statement:

> 15 And he said unto them, Go ye into all the world, and preach the gospel to every creature.
> 16 He that believeth and is baptized shall be saved; but he that believeth not shall be damned. (Mark, Chapter 16)

This remark has often been a justification for Christians arguing that the Christian religion is the only road to salvation. It has been a major justification for the aggressive and violent behavior of Christians ever since they gained military might through the formation of the Roman Catholic Church.

15 | What Is Truth?

We now see a deeper meaning, namely that the true gospel of Christ is the Gospel of Oneness. It is this gospel – the "good news" that oneness is the underlying reality and that division is an illusion created by the devil – that Jesus wants preached to all the world. It is those who accept this gospel who will be saved by entering the kingdom of God, namely the Christ consciousness. Those who reject the Gospel of Oneness will be damned to remaining in the consciousness of separation where there is weeping and gnashing of teeth because you are constantly in opposition to someone.

We now see that we cannot consider the written words as the ultimate expression of Christ. We need to go beyond the written words and avoid interpreting them through the ego, the separate self. We need to use the words only as a stepping stone for reaching the Spirit behind the words, the Spirit from which the words originated. We need to live up to the following statement:

> But the hour cometh, and now is, when the true worshippers shall worship the Father in spirit and in truth: for the Father seeketh such to worship him. (John 2:22)

Mainstream Christians have had 2,000 years to stop taking the same approach to Jesus' words as the scribes and Pharisees. That's long enough and I for one am not going to wait for them any longer, nor will I remain silent in order to avoid offending them.

Words and the Spirit

I earlier talked about the fact that Jesus did not write down his teachings, and we can now gain a deeper understanding. Jesus knew that there is a difference between the written word and the spoken word. We all know this because we have experienced how a person can yell at us: "You're so stupid!!!" And the words carry an energy that hits us in a different way than when we read those same words.

Why did people feel that Jesus taught them with authority and not as the scribes? The scribes were the intellectuals of their day and they likely talked like the scientists or theologians of today. They attempted to give reasoned arguments that appealed to the intellect. As we can see from the endless theological debates over subtle points in the interpretation of scripture, the intellect can argue for or against any point without coming up with a decisive view. The words of intellectuals carry no authority because they are not beyond argumentation.

Why did Jesus teach with "authority?" He had attained the Christ consciousness and when he spoke, the universal Christ consciousness was flowing through his words, infusing them with Spirit. It was by encountering this flow of Spirit that the people realized there was something different about Jesus. Through the combination of words and Spirit, their inner ability to recognize Christ was activated.

Jesus knew that the flow of the Spirit can be conveyed in fullness only through the spoken word and not through the written word. He attempted to establish a movement where people would speak by being the open doors for the comforter, the Holy Spirit. They would therefore be able to convey more through the spoken word than could be conveyed through the written word. This would reduce the risk that people would use words to increase division and conflict. They would not be divided over the interpretation of written words, but would be united in experiencing the Spirit flowing through the Living Word.

As I have argued, this tradition of the comforter was lost, and instead we see the emergence of a church that selected a group of written gospels, and then elevated them to the status of being the ultimate authority on the Word of Christ. Christians have been interpreting those fixed words ever since.

This doesn't mean I am saying that the written word is useless and we should throw out the Bible. If I thought so, it would be kind of contradictory to state so through the written word, wouldn't it? The written word can indeed promote our growth in consciousness, but only if we understand the need to go beyond the intellectual mind and reach for an inner experience of the Spirit. Most of us have probably had the experience of reading something and suddenly we feel this inner sensation or stirring, giving us an Aha Experience that is beyond intellectual understanding. We don't simply understand a point, we "see" it and we experience its reality.

We now see a basic fact. Written scriptures or teachings have value only if we use them as a tool for having an experience of the Spirit. The question now becomes: "Which spirit do we experience?"

The Spirit versus spirits

I have met many Christians who have had an experience of encountering the Spirit while reading the Bible. You can find people – especially in evangelical circles – who claim that they have had powerful experiences of the Spirit showing them that the Bible is the infallible word of God and that Christianity is the only road to salvation.

I am not trying to denounce all such experiences, but I am encouraging a certain discernment. You can find people who claim that the Spirit showed them the infallible truth of a particular interpretation of the Bible. You can find two people who both claim to have been shown an infallible interpretation of scripture, but when you compare them, they are incompatible. How do we explain that? Jesus was trying to show us that behind all of the appearances in this world there is one underlying reality, namely the Christ consciousness. This shows us that reality is one interconnected and indivisible whole. We can therefore say that behind all diversity there is one Spirit, namely an indivisible Spirit of Oneness, the Holy Spirit. If you are able to make contact with that Spirit, it will give you a direct experience of the fact that oneness is the only reality and that separation is an illusion.

Take note that this does not mean that everyone will have the same experience. As I have said, we are at different levels of consciousness and we all have a number of illusions we need to overcome in order to enter the consciousness of oneness. The goal of the Holy Spirit is not to take me in one giant leap to oneness. The goal is to take me one step closer, and to continue doing so as long as I am willing.

We now see one explanation for the phenomenon that different people have different experiences. Say I have an experience of the Spirit while reading the Bible. This helps me see the fallacy of one of my beliefs and I let go of that illusion. Yet I am not ready to let go of certain other illusions to which I am still very attached. It is now possible that since I had the experience while reading the Bible, I can interpret this to mean that while the Spirit helped me see through one illusion, the reality of the experience confirmed either the validity of the Bible or of certain other beliefs.

What have I now done? I have used an experience of the Spirit to overcome one illusion but to solidify another illusion. I have thereby closed my mind to the possibility that the Spirit could – when I was ready for it – show me the need to abandon another illusion. I have met Christians who had what I believe was a genuine experience of the Spirit, but they have interpreted it as a validation of their particular Christian beliefs, thereby closing their minds to any experience that could take them beyond those beliefs. Why is this a problem? What did Jesus say about the Spirit:

> The wind bloweth where it listeth, and thou hearest the sound thereof, but canst not tell whence it cometh, and whither it goeth: so is every one that is born of the Spirit. (John, 3:8)

The fact that the Spirit "bloweth where it listeth" means that it will not conform to beliefs and expectations based on the mind of anti-christ, the consciousness of separation. The true Holy Spirit has only one goal and that is to take us to the fullness of the Christ consciousness. This means we must overcome *all* of the illusions of anti-christ, all of the serpentine lies. Does that mean we need to question *all* of our beliefs? Well, one thing I can say for sure: We have to *be willing* to question all of our beliefs. Any belief that we are not wiling to question becomes a barrier to the Holy Spirit, and that could very well cause us to reject Christ. We will follow him so far, but there is still a belief that we will not question, a part of the human self that we are not willing to let die.

But why not go all the way? I have argued that the fullness of "The Word" cannot be captured in "words." In order to attain complete oneness with Christ, we have to go beyond *all* beliefs that can be formulated in words and attain oneness, gnosis, with the Spirit of Oneness. We now see that being a follower of Christ means that we are constantly alert to the possibility that something in our own minds can act as an instrument for the consciousness of separation and cause us to reject taking another step towards oneness. The only real question is: "Does it take me closer to oneness or does it keep me in separation?"

To complete this section, we also need to consider that Jesus cast out spirits from people. There are indeed lower spirits that spring from the consciousness of separation. These spirits are capable of giving people an experience that can feel very powerful and very real. When a Muslim has an experience that makes him believe God has called him to strap on a bomb and blow himself up in a public bus in Jerusalem, that experience might have seemed very powerful and real to him, but was it an experience of the Holy Spirit? How could it be when it caused him to destroy another part of life, thereby tying himself to the consciousness of the devil, the consciousness that sees itself as a god who can decide who will live or die?

Most Christians will probably agree with this, but is it because they think Islam is a false religion, or is it because they see the deeper reality that separation is an illusion? A Christian crusader may have had a very powerful and seemingly real experience that he thought justified him killing Muslims. It might indeed have been a genuine experience, but did it come from the Holy Spirit or from one of the spirits of separation?

It really is quite simple. Any experience that takes us closer to oneness comes from the Holy Spirit. Any experience that keeps us in separation or takes us deeper into separation comes from a lesser spirit.

What about truth?

I know you can say: "You are saying that even though Jesus wasn't the only son of God, he was the Christ incarnate and he came to set us free by giving us truth. Doesn't that mean his words were true?" The deeper reality is that no words are true in and of themselves; it is what we do with them that makes them true or false.

15 | What Is Truth?

When Jesus walked among us, he used words for the purpose of helping us transcend specific illusions and take us one step closer to oneness. If we use his words that way today, then those words are true in us. If, on the other hand, we interpret his words through the separate self and use them as weapons against other people, seeking to prove ourselves superior by proving other people wrong, then Jesus' words are not true in us. We have made them false by using them to affirm the illusion of separation. Take a look at a very telling statement where Jesus is again confronting the scribes and Pharisees:

> Making the word of God of none effect through your tradition, which ye have delivered: (Mark, 7:13)

What Jesus is exposing here is that the human ego – and the forces of anti-christ – have a tendency to create a "tradition" for how the "word of God" should be interpreted. When the Living Christ or the Holy Spirit gives them the Living Word, they use their dead word as a justification for rejecting it, as Peter rejected Jesus.

When Jesus spoke his words 2,000 years ago, those words carried the Spirit of Truth. Thus, they did carry the vibration of truth. If you use a man-made tradition – no matter how much authority it claims to have – to reject the Living Word that Jesus and the Holy Spirit are willing to give you directly in your heart, you are making the word of God of no effect through your tradition.

The very claim that Christianity is the only true religion and the only road to salvation is a direct creation of the mind of anti-christ. This belief will inevitably create a division between those who believe it and those who don't. The true religion and the only road to salvation is the consciousness of Christ, the consciousness of oneness. Many take the broad way – the divided way – that leads to destruction. Few find the strait and narrow way, the undivided way, of Christ. I think that in today's age more people than ever are ready for the inner path of oneness. I hope this book will help some connect their inner readiness with outer awareness and acceptance.

16 | THE SECOND COMING OF CHRIST

Will Jesus come back to save us?

Millions of Christians around the world are waiting for an event often called "the second coming of Christ." Although the specifics vary, the core of this belief is that at some time in the near future (millions of Christians believe it will happen in their lifetime), Jesus will come back to earth in a second coming that will be an undeniable sign. He will then take the faithful (sometimes defined as the membership of a small church) to heaven, will condemn all non-believers to hell and will destroy the entire universe.

An American minister has set specific dates to this event—twice. He first said Jesus would return on September 6, 1994. After taking some time to recover from the failure of this prophecy, he predicted that it would occur on May 21, 2011 with the final destruction of the world on October 21, 2011. Of course, New Age people are likewise into a variety of prophecies, and many believed that a similarly dramatic event would take place on December 21, 2012 with the end of the Mayan calendar.

Based on everything we have discussed, we can see that this entire idea is a product of the consciousness of separation that leads to the belief in an external savior. In reality, Jesus will not come back to save us, nor will we be saved by aliens in spaceships or the great pumpkin man. The only thing that will save us from ourselves is the Christ within ourselves.

The second coming of Christ is *not* an event where Jesus will physically or visibly return to earth. It is an event where the universal Christ consciousness will take embodiment in and through a large number of people. The true second coming of Christ is the awakening of the Christ in many of us!

If Jesus did indeed come back, it would work directly against his true goals. Just look at how his first coming has been used to claim the Christ could appear only in him, thereby denying it in all of us. Do you think he would add fuel to that fire by appearing again?

On the contrary, Jesus has been in embodiment on earth and he has played his role. He came to be an example, and if there is to be a second coming of Christ, it must be because millions of us dare to embrace the Christ consciousness directly within ourselves instead of continuing to project it outside ourselves. We are the ones who are in embodiment today and it is our turn to play the role of the Christ.

Is Jesus no longer needed?

I know some will say it sounds like I think Jesus is no longer needed or that he is no longer significant. On the contrary, I think Jesus is a pivotal figure in the spiritual life of earth. I think Jesus is a living spiritual being today, an ascended being or ascended master. I think he is very much still involved with

16 | The Second Coming of Christ

seeking to raise the consciousness of humankind and that he is willing to work with and through those who dare become the open doors.

I also think there is a hierarchy of spiritual beings and that they occupy various offices. I believe Jesus represents the Christ consciousness for planet earth by holding the office of the planetary Christ.

I realize that for many people who have given up on Christianity, the word "Christ" has a sectarian ring. I see it as a universal word that has been hijacked by a non-universal religion. I think it is indeed true that no one can ascend to the spiritual realm without attaining the Christ consciousness. I also think this simply cannot happen unless we work with and go through the spiritual office held by the ascended master Jesus. Thus, it is actually true in a spiritual sense that Jesus is the way, the truth and the life. None of us — no matter what outer religion we follow — will come to the father without going through Jesus and his spiritual office.

I have met many New Age or spiritual people who have rejected Jesus because they cannot separate him from the doctrines and actions of the Christian religion. I fully understand that sentiment, but I don't think serious spiritual seekers can afford to have it. I think all of us need to acknowledge that we chose to be born in a situation where we would be exposed to mainstream Christianity in one form or another. We chose to do this because at higher levels of our beings, we know that we have to overcome our aversion to Christianity and make peace with Jesus as an ascended master.

I have personally made a determined effort to see beyond Christianity and make peace with Jesus as a living spiritual Being. I hope this book can help you find an inner resolution so you know exactly what role the ascended master Jesus plays in your life. May the second coming of Christ happen in you.

I hope this book can help you find
an inner resolution so you know exactly
what role the ascended master Jesus
plays in your life.

✤

EPILOGUE

For those who accept at least some of the ideas I have presented in this book, what should happen next? Should they leave existing Christian churches? Should they seek to reform their church? Should they form a new organization based on the mystical path of Christ?

I have no answer to these questions because I don't think there is a single answer. For the past 36 years I have done everything in my power to walk the mystical path of Christ. During this process I have come to accept Christ within myself and I have allowed it to express itself in ways that often surprised me. In going through this process, I have not come to see myself as a kind of prophet or leader that others should follow. On the contrary, by recognizing the Christ in myself, I have also recognized that Christ is in all other people.

I am an instrument for bringing forth ideas about the inner path of Christ. I am not an instrument for telling others how they should implement these ideas in their personal lives or in their churches. Why not? Because what *you* should do with these ideas is not a matter of following anyone outside yourself. It is a matter of what the Christ in you wants to do through you.

The Christ is in all of us, meaning that we can all make contact with the comforter sent by Jesus and available to us today. Jesus does not want me to tell you what to do, he does not want to tell you through me. He wants to tell you directly in your own heart. My role is to be an instrument for revealing the inner path that can empower you to make your own direct, inner connection with the comforter, with the Christ consciousness and with Jesus.

In me, the Christ has so far desired to express itself in bringing forth ideas about the inner path. It has done so in this book, in other books and I assume it will do so in future books. The questions for you are: "How does the Christ want to express itself through me? How does the universal Christ consciousness want to be individualized in me?" I hope this book and my other books will help you find your personal answers to those questions.

As a final note, I earlier talked about how we can use even the scriptures to prove certain beliefs or validate the intentions of the outer self. I am well aware that one can say that in this book I have taken selected quotes from the scriptures and used them to prove my point. You might disagree with my use of the scriptures in general or with specific points I am making. I have only one response. I have written this book in the Spirit of Oneness, as far as I am able to grasp it at this moment. I sincerely believe that if you read this book with the Spirit of Oneness, it will not lead you astray but will take you closer to oneness.

About the Author

Kim Michaels has written over 25 books on topics related to spirituality, mysticism and self-help. He has conducted spiritual conferences and workshops in 14 countries, has counseled hundreds of spiritual students and has done numerous radio shows on spiritual topics. Kim has been on the spiritual path since 1976. He has studied a wide variety of spiritual teachings and practiced many techniques for raising consciousness. He has developed a particular expertise concerning the mystical teachings of Jesus and the practice of Christian mysticism. For personal information, visit Kim at *www.KimMichaels.info*.

www.ingramcontent.com/pod-product-compliance
Lightning Source LLC
Chambersburg PA
CBHW021147160426
43194CB00007B/728